# YOUR
# HOR
# 2012

♉

# TAURUS

# YOUR PERSONAL
# HOROSCOPE
# 2012

# TAURUS

21st April–21st May

*igloo*

This edition published by Igloo Books Ltd,
Cottage Farm, Sywell, Northants NN6 0BJ
www.igloo-books.com

Produced for Igloo Books by W. Foulsham & Co. Ltd,
Capital Point, 33 Bath Road, Slough, Berkshire, SL1 3UF, England

ISBN: 9780857349453

This is an abridged version of material
originally published in *Old Moore's Horoscope
and Astral Diary*.

Printed and manufactured in China

# CONTENTS

# INTRODUCTION

Your Personal Horoscopes have been specifically created to allow you to get the most from astrological patterns and the way they have a bearing on not only your zodiac sign, but nuances within it. Using the diary section of the book you can read about the influences and possibilities of each and every day of the year. It will be possible for you to see when you are likely to be cheerful and happy or those times when your nature is in retreat and you will be more circumspect. The diary will help to give you a feel for the specific 'cycles' of astrology and the way they can subtly change your day-to-day life. For example, when you see the sign ☿, this means that the planet Mercury is retrograde at that time. Retrograde means it appears to be running backwards through the zodiac. Such a happening has a significant effect on communication skills, but this is only one small aspect of how the Personal Horoscope can help you.

With Your Personal Horoscope the story doesn't end with the diary pages. It includes simple ways for you to work out the zodiac sign the Moon occupied at the time of your birth, and what this means for your personality. In addition, if you know the time of day you were born, it is possible to discover your Ascendant, yet another important guide to your personal make-up and potential.

Many readers are interested in relationships and in knowing how well they get on with people of other astrological signs. You might also be interested in the way you appear to very different sorts of individuals. If you are such a person, the section on Venus will be of particular interest. Despite the rapidly changing position of this planet, you can work out your Venus sign, and learn what bearing it will have on your life.

Using Your Personal Horoscope you can travel on one of the most fascinating and rewarding journeys that anyone can take – the journey to a better realisation of self.

# THE ESSENCE
# OF TAURUS

## *Exploring the Personality of*
## *Taurus the Bull*

### (21ST APRIL – 21ST MAY)

## What's in a sign?

Taurus is probably one of the most misunderstood signs of the zodiac. Astrologers from the past described those born under the sign of the Bull as being gentle, artistic, stubborn and refined. All of this is quite true, but there is so much more to Taureans and the only reason it isn't always discussed as much as it should be is because of basic Taurean reserve. Taureans are generally modest, and don't tend to assert themselves in a direct sense, unless in self-defence. As a result the sign is often sidelined, if not ignored.

You know what you want from life and are quite willing to work long and hard to get it. However, Taurus is also a great lover of luxury, so when circumstances permit you can be slow, ponderous and even lax. If there is a paradox here it is merely typical of Venus-ruled Taurus. On differing occasions you can be chatty or quiet, bold or timorous, smart or scruffy. It all depends on your commitment to a situation. When you are inspired there is nobody powerful enough to hold you back and when you are passionate you have the proclivities of a Casanova!

There are aspects of your nature that seldom change. For example, you are almost always friendly and approachable, and invariably have a sense of what feels and looks just right. You are capable and can work with your hands as well as your brain. You don't particularly care for dirt or squalid surroundings, preferring cleanliness, and you certainly don't take kindly to abject poverty. Most Taureans prefer the country to the coast, find loving relationships easy to deal with and are quite committed to home and family.

Whilst variety is the spice of life to many zodiac signs this is not necessarily the case for Taurus. Many people born under the sign of the Bull remain happy to occupy a specific position for years on end. It has been suggested, with more than a grain of truth, that the only thing that can get the Bull moving on occasions is a strategically placed bomb. What matters most, and which shows regularly in your dealings with the world at large, is your innate kindness and your desire to help others.

## Taurus resources

The best word to describe Taurean subjects who are working to the best of their ability would be 'practical'. Nebulous situations, where you have to spend long hours thinking things through in a subconscious manner, don't suit you half as much as practical tasks, no matter how complex these might be. If you were to find yourself cast up on a desert island you would have all the necessities of life sorted out in a flash. This is not to suggest that you always recognise this potential in yourself. The problem here is that a very definite lack of self-belief is inclined to make you think that almost anyone else in the world has the edge when it comes to talent.

Another of your greatest resources is your creative potential. You always have the knack of knowing what looks and feels just right. This is as true when it comes to decorating your home as it is regarding matters out there in the big, wide world. If this skill could be allied to confidence on a regular basis, there would be little or nothing to stop you. You may well possess specific skills which others definitely don't have, and you get on best when these are really needed.

Taureans don't mind dealing with routine matters and you have a good administrative ability in a number of different fields. With a deeply intuitive streak (when you are willing to recognise it), it isn't usually hard for you to work out how any particular individual would react under given circumstances. Where you fall down on occasions is that you don't always recognise the great advantages that are yours for the taking, and self-belief could hardly be considered the Taurean's greatest virtue.

Taurus people are good at making lists, even if these are of the mental variety. Your natural warmth makes it possible for you to find friends where others would not, and the sort of advice that you offer is considered and sensible. People feel they can rely on you, a fact that could prove to be one of the most important of your resources. There is nothing at all wrong with using this ability to feather your own nest, particularly since you are not the sort of person who would willingly stand on those around you in order to get where you want to go.

# Beneath the surface

To say that you are deep would be a definite understatement. Only you know how far down into the basement some of your considerations and emotions actually go. Because you exhibit a generally practical face to the world at large the true scope of the Taurean mind remains something of a mystery to those around you. Certainly you seem to be uncomplicated and even a little superficial at times, though nothing could be further from the truth. Very little happens to you that fails to be filed away in some recess or other of that great interior that is your mind's library. It may be because of this that Taurus is well known for being able to bear a grudge for a long time. However, what is sometimes forgotten is that you never let a kindness from someone else go without reward, even though it may take you a very long time to find a way to say thank you.

Affairs of the heart are of special importance to you and ties of the romantic kind go as deep as any emotion. Once you love you tend to do so quite unconditionally. It takes months or years of upsets to shake your faith in love, and it's a fact that even in these days of marital splits, Taureans are far more likely than most signs of the zodiac to remain hitched. The simple fact is that you believe in loyalty, absolutely and irrevocably. The thought of letting anyone down once you have given your word is almost unthinkable and if such a situation does occur there are almost always quite definite mitigating factors.

Rules and regulations are easy for you to deal with because you have a natural tendency to order. You are also fairly good at dealing with routines and probably have your own life well sorted out as a result. A word of caution is necessary only when this internal need for order extends too much into your external life. Taureans can be fanatical about having a tidy house or for making things work out exactly as they would wish in a work sense. These tendencies start within the recesses of your own, often closed, mind. The way forward here is to throw open the doors and windows now and again and to let those around you know how you function internally. It isn't easy, because you are quite a closed book at heart. However the exercise is well worthwhile and the results can be quite breathtaking.

## Making the best of yourself

Anyone who wants to work to the best of their ability first needs a good deal of self-knowledge. In your case this means recognising just what you are capable of doing and then concentrating in these directions. Of course it's only human nature to be all the things we are not, but this tendency runs deeper in you than it does in the majority of individuals. Use your natural kindness to the full and ally this to your practical ability to get things done. Sorting things out is easy for you, so easy in fact that you sometimes fail to realise that not everyone has these skills to the same extent.

Confidence definitely seems to be evident in the way you deal with the world at large. Of course you know that this often isn't the case, but that doesn't matter. It's the way the world at large views you that counts, so keep moving forward, even on those occasions when you are shaking inside. Use your naturally creative skills to the full and cultivate that innate sense of order in ways that benefit you and the world at a very practical level.

Avoid the tendency to be stubborn by convincing yourself that so many things 'simply don't matter'. An inability to move, simply because you feel annoyed or aggrieved, is certainly going to be more of a hindrance than a help – though there are occasions when, like all facets of nature, it's essential. Cultivate the more cheerful qualities that are endemic to your nature and be prepared to mix freely with as many different sorts of people as you possibly can. Be willing to take on new responsibilities because the more you are able to do so, the greater is your natural sense of self-worth. Stitching all these qualities together and using them to your own advantage isn't always easy, but pays handsomely in the end.

## The impressions you give

This is a very interesting section as far as the sign of Taurus is concerned. The reason is very simply that you fail on so many occasions to betray the sheer depth of your own Earth-sign nature. That doesn't mean to say that you come across badly to others. On the contrary, you are probably a very popular person, except with those people who mistreat or cheat others. You have a great sense of what is right, and don't tend to deviate from a point of view once you've come to terms with it.

The world sees you as capable, cheerful and generally active, though with a tendency to be sluggish and lethargic on occasions. Perhaps Taurus needs to explain itself more because even when you are not at your most vibrant best there are invariably reasons. You can be quite secretive, though only usually about yourself. This can make life with the Taurean something of a guessing game on occasions. Certainly you appear to be much more fixed in your attitude than might often be the case. Why should this be so? It's mainly because you do have extremely definite ideas about specific matters, and since you sometimes display these it's natural that others pigeon-hole you as a very 'definite' sort. Actually this is far from being the whole truth but, once again, if you don't explain yourself, others can be left in the dark.

You almost certainly are not short of friends. People recognise that you are friendly, tolerant and extremely supportive. You give the impression of being very trustworthy and people know that they can rely on you to act in a specific manner. If this appears to make you somewhat predictable it doesn't really matter because you are deeply loved, and that's what counts. One fact is almost certain – the world has a greater regard for you in a general sense than you have for yourself.

## The way forward

The ideal life for the Taurus subject seems to be one that is settled and happy, with not too much upheaval and plenty of order. Whether or not this truly turns out to be the case depends on a number of factors. For starters, even those born under the sign of the Bull have a boredom threshold. This means that having to respond to change and diversity probably does you more good than you might at first think. At the same time you won't know exactly what you are capable of doing unless you really stretch yourself, and that's something that you are not always willing to do.

You do function best from within loving relationships, and although you can be very passionate, once you have given your heart you don't tend to change your mind readily. Personal and domestic contentment are worth a great deal to you because they represent the platform upon which you build the rest of your life. You don't make a good itinerant and probably won't indulge in travel for its own sake. Of course it does you good to get around, since anything that broadens your horizons has got to be an advantage, but you'll probably always maintain a solid home base and relish the prospect of coming back to it as frequently as possible.

Most Taureans are family people. You can be a capable parent, though tend to be a little more authoritarian than some types. Keeping an ordered sort of life is at the base of your psychology, so that even when you are young and less tidy-minded there is always a basic desire for self-discipline. This often extends to your work, where you are extremely capable and can quite easily work under your own supervision. You recognise the beautiful in all spheres of life and tend to gravitate towards clean and sanitary surroundings.

In matters of health you tend to be fairly robust, though you can suffer somewhat with headaches, often brought about as a result of a stiff neck and stress. This latter is what you should avoid as much as possible. Saying what you feel, and listening carefully to the responses, is definitely of great importance. The more you learn, the wiser you become. This makes you the natural resort of others when they need help and advice. If you try not to underestimate your own abilities, you can rise as far in life as the world at large thinks you are capable of doing. At the end of the day it is important to recognise your popularity. In all probability your friends have a much higher opinion of you than the one you cultivate for yourself.

# TAURUS ON THE CUSP

Astrological profiles are altered for those people born at either the beginning or the end of a zodiac sign, or, more properly, on the cusps of a sign. In the case of Taurus this would be on the 21st of April and for two or three days after, and similarly at the end of the sign, probably from the 18th to the 21st of May.

## The Aries Cusp – April 21st to April 24th

Although you have all the refinement, breeding and creative flair of the true Taurean, you are definitely more of a go-getter. Knowing what you want from life there is a slight possibility that you might be accused of being bossy and sometimes this slightly hurts your Taurean sensitivity. You have plenty of energy to get through the things that you see as being important but it is quite possible that those around you don't always see things in the same light, and this can be annoying to you. Like the typical Taurean you have great reserves of energy and can work long and hard towards any particular objective although, because Aries is also in attendance, you may push yourself slightly harder than is strictly necessary. Your temper is variable and you may not always display the typical Taurean patience with those around you.

It is possible for Taurus to 'wait in the wings' deliberately and therefore to lose out on some of the most important potential gains as a result. In your case, this is much less likely. You don't worry too much about speaking your mind. You are loving and kind, but even family members know that they will only be able to push you so far. At work, you are capable and have executive ability. Like the Taurean you don't really care for getting your hands dirty, but if needs must you can pitch in with the best of them and enjoy a challenge. You don't worry as much as some of your Taurean friends do, but all the same you regularly expect too much of your nervous system and need frequent periods of rest.

Try not to impose your will on those around you and be content to allow things to happen on their own sometimes. This might not be an easy thing for the Aries-cusp Taurean but it's one of the sure ways to success. Confidence isn't lacking and neither is basic patience, but they do have to be encouraged and nurtured.

# The Gemini Cusp – May 18th to May 21st

Oh, what a happy person you are – and how much the world loves you for it! This is definitely the more potentially fortunate of the two Taurean cusps, or at least that is how the majority of the people who know you would view it. The fact is that you are bright and breezy, easygoing and sometimes fickle on occasions, but supporting these trends is a patient, generally contented attitude to life that is both refreshing and inspiring. Getting others on your side is not hard and you have plenty of energy when it is needed the most. All the same you are quite capable of dozing in the sun occasionally and probably put far less stress on your nervous system than either Taurus or Gemini when taken alone.

You don't care too much for routines and you love variety, but yet you retain the creative and artistic qualities that come with the sign of the Bull. You work well and with confidence, but would be very likely to change direction in your career at some stage in your life and are not half so tied to routine as is usually the case for Taurus. With a friendly, and even a passionate, approach to matters of the heart you are an attentive lover and a fond parent. Most people know what you really are because you are only too willing to show them. Working out the true motivations that lurk within your soul is part of your personal search to know 'self' and is extremely important.

All in all, you have exactly what it takes to get on in life and a sense of joy and fun that makes you good to know. Patience balances your need to 'get going', whilst your mischievous streak lightens the load of the sign of Taurus which can, on occasions, take itself rather more seriously than it should.

There are many ways of coping with the requirements of life and, at one time or another, it is likely that you will try them all out. But above and beyond your need to experiment you know what is most important to you and that will always be your ultimate goal. What matters the most is your smile, which is enduring and even alluring.

# TAURUS AND ITS ASCENDANTS

The nature of every individual on the planet is composed of the rich variety of zodiac signs and planetary positions that were present at the time of their birth. Your Sun sign, which in your case is Taurus, is one of the many factors when it comes to assessing the unique person you are. Probably the most important consideration, other than your Sun sign, is to establish the zodiac sign that was rising over the eastern horizon at the time that you were born. This is your Ascending or Rising sign. Most popular astrology fails to take account of the Ascendant, and yet its importance remains with you from the very moment of your birth, through every day of your life. The Ascendant is evident in the way you approach the world, and so, when meeting a person for the first time, it is this astrological influence that you are most likely to notice first. Our Ascending sign essentially represents what we appear to be, while the Sun sign is what we feel inside ourselves.

The Ascendant also has the potential for modifying our overall nature. For example, if you were born at a time of day when Taurus was passing over the eastern horizon (this would be around the time of dawn) then you would be classed as a double Taurus. As such, you would typify this zodiac sign, both internally and in your dealings with others. However, if your Ascendant sign turned out to be a Fire sign, such as Leo, there would be a profound alteration of nature, away from the expected qualities of Taurus.

One of the reasons why popular astrology often ignores the Ascendant is that it has always been rather difficult to establish. We have found a way to make this possible by devising an easy-to-use table, which you will find on page 157 of this book. Using this, you can establish your Ascendant sign at a glance. You will need to know your rough time of birth, then it is simply a case of following the instructions.

For those readers who have no idea of their time of birth it might be worth allowing a good friend, or perhaps your partner, to read through the section that follows this introduction. Someone who deals with you on a regular basis may easily discover your Ascending sign, even though you could have some difficulty establishing it for yourself. A good understanding of this component of your nature is essential if you want to be aware of that 'other person' who is responsible for the way you make contact with the world at large.

Your Sun sign, Ascendant sign, and the other pointers in this book will, together, allow you a far better understanding of what makes you tick as an individual. Peeling back the different layers of your astrological make-up can be an enlightening experience, and the Ascendant may represent one of the most important layers of all.

## Taurus with Taurus Ascendant

The world would see you as being fairly typical of the sign of Taurus, so you are careful, sensitive, well bred and, if other astrological trends agree, very creative. Nothing pleases you more than a tidy environment to live in and a peaceful life. You probably believe that there is a place for everything and will do your best to keep it all where it should be. It's a pity that this sometimes includes people, and you are certain to get rather irritated if they don't behave in the way that you would expect. Despite this, you are generally understanding and are very capable of giving and receiving affection.

Not everyone knows the real you, however, and it is sometimes difficult to tell the world those most personal details that can be locked deep inside. At an emotional level you tend to idealise love somewhat, though if anything this presents itself to the world as a slight 'coldness' on occasions. This is far from the truth, but your tidy mind demands that even the most intimate processes are subjected to the same sense of order with which you view the world at large. Unlike many sign combinations, you don't really rely on the help and support of others because you are more than capable yourself. In the main you live a happy life and have the ability to pass on this trait to those you care for.

18

# Taurus with Gemini Ascendant

This is a generally happy combination which finds you better able to externalise the cultured and creative qualities which are inherent in your Taurean nature. You love to be around interesting and stimulating people and tend to be much more talkative than the typical Taurean is expected to be. The reason why Gemini helps here is because it lightens the load somewhat. Taurus is not the most introspective sign of the zodiac, but it does have that quality, and a good dose of Gemini allows you to speak your mind more freely and, as a result, to know yourself better too.

Although your mind tends to be fairly logical, you also enjoy flashes of insight that can cause you to behave in a less rational way from time to time. This is probably no bad thing because life will never be boring with you around. You try to convince yourself that you take on board all the many and varied opinions that come back at you from others, though there is a slight danger of intellectual snobbery if the responses you get are not the expected ones. You particularly like clean houses, funny people and probably fast cars. Financial rewards can come thick and fast to the Gemini-Ascendant Taurean when the logical but inspirational mind is harnessed to practical matters.

## Taurus with Cancer Ascendant

Your main aim in life seems to be to look after everyone and everything that you come across. From your deepest and most enduring human love, right down to the birds in the park, you really do care and you show that natural affection in a thousand different ways. Your nature is sensitive and you are easily moved to tears, though this does not prevent you from pitching in and doing practical things to assist at just about any level. There is a danger that you could stifle those same people whom you set out to assist, and people with this zodiac combination are often unwilling, or unable, to allow their children to grow and leave the nest. More time spent considering what suits you would be no bad thing, but the problem is that you find it almost impossible to imagine any situation that doesn't involve your most basic need, which is to nurture.

You appear not to possess a selfish streak, though it sometimes turns out that, in being certain that you understand the needs and wants of the world, you are nevertheless treading on their toes. This eventual realisation can be very painful, but it isn't a stick with which you should beat yourself because at heart you are one of the kindest people imaginable. Your sense of fair play means that you are a quiet social reformer at heart.

# Taurus with Leo Ascendant

Oh dear, this can be rather a hedonistic combination. The trouble is that Taurus tends to have a great sense of what looks and feels right, whilst Leo, being a Cat, is inclined to preen itself on almost any occasion. The combination tends towards self-love, which is all too likely for someone who is perfect. But don't be too dispirited about these facts because there is a great deal going for you in other ways. For a start you have one of the warmest hearts to be found anywhere and you are so brave that others marvel at the courage you display. The mountains that you climb may not be of the large, rocky sort, but you manage to find plenty of pinnacles to scale all the same, and you invariably get to the top.

Routines might bore you a little more than would be the case with Taurus alone, but you don't mind being alone. Why should you? You are probably the nicest person you know! Thus if you were ever to be cast up on a deserted island you would people the place all on your own, and there would never be any crime, untidiness or arguments. Problems only arise when other people are involved. However, in social settings you are charming, good to know and full of ideas that really have legs. You preserve your youth well into middle age, but at base you can tend to worry more than is good for you.

# Taurus with Virgo Ascendant

This combination tends to amplify the Taurean qualities that you naturally possess and this is the case because both Taurus and Virgo are Earth signs. However, there are certain factors related to Virgo that show themselves very differently than the sign's cousin Taurus. Virgo is more fussy, nervy and and pedantic than Taurus and all of these qualities are going to show up in your nature at one level or another. On the plus side, you might be slightly less concerned about having a perfect home and a perfect family, and your interest in life appears at a more direct level than that of the true Taurean. You care very much about your home and family and are very loyal to your friends. It's true that you sometimes tend to try and take them over, and you can also show a marked tendency to dominate, but your heart is in the right place, and most people recognise that your caring is genuine.

One problem is that there are very few shades of grey in your life, which is certainly not the case for other zodiac sign combinations. Living your life in the way that you do, there isn't much room for compromise, and this fact alone can prove to be something of a problem where relationships are concerned. In a personal sense you need a partner who is willing to be organised and one who relies heavily on your judgements, which don't change very often.

# Taurus with Libra Ascendant

A fortunate combination in many ways, this is a double Venus rulership, since both Taurus and Libra are heavily reliant on the planet of love. You are social, amiable and a natural diplomat, anxious to please and ready to care for just about anyone who shows interest in you. You hate disorder, which means that there is a place for everything and everything in its place. This can throw up the odd paradox, however, since being half Libran you cannot always work out where that place ought to be! You deal with life in a humorous way and are quite capable of seeing the absurd in yourself, as well as in others. Your heart is no bigger than that of the dyed-in-the-wool Taurean, but it sits rather closer to the surface and so others recognise it more.

On those occasions when you know you are standing on firm ground you can show great confidence, even if you have to be ready to change some of your opinions at the drop of a hat. When this happens you can be quite at odds with yourself, because Taurus doesn't take very many U-turns, whereas Libra does. Don't expect to know yourself too well, and keep looking for the funny side of things, because it is within humour that you forge the sort of life that suits you best.

# Taurus with Scorpio Ascendant

The first, last and most important piece of advice for you is not to take yourself, or anyone else, too seriously. This might be rather a tall order because Scorpio intensifies the deeper qualities of Taurus and can make you rather lacking in the sense of humour that we all need to live our lives in this most imperfect of worlds. You are naturally sensuous by nature. This shows itself in a host of ways. In all probability you can spend hours in the bath, love to treat yourself to good food and drink and take your greatest pleasure in neat and orderly surroundings. On occasions this can alienate you from those who live in the same house, because other people do need to use the bathroom from time to time, and they cannot remain tidy indefinitely.

You tend to worry a great deal about things which are really not very important, but don't take this statement too seriously or you will begin to worry about this, too! You often need to lighten up and should always do your best to tell yourself that most things are not half so important as they seem to be. Be careful over the selection of a life partner and if possible choose someone who is naturally funny and who does not take life anywhere near as seriously as you are inclined to do. At work you are more than capable and in all probability everyone relies heavily on your wise judgements.

# Taurus with Sagittarius Ascendant

A dual nature is evident here, and if it doesn't serve to confuse you, it will certainly be a cause of concern to many of the people with whom you share your life. You like to have a good time and are a natural party-goer. On such occasions you are accommodating, chatty and good to know. But contrast this with the quieter side of Taurus, which is directly opposed to your Sagittarian qualities. The opposition of forces is easy for you to deal with because you inhabit your own body and mind all the time, but it's far less easy for friends and relatives to understand. So on those occasions when you decide that, socially speaking, enough is enough, you may have trouble explaining this to the twelve people who are waiting outside your door with party hats and whoopee cushions.

Confidence to do almost anything is not far from the forefront of your mind and you readily embark on adventures that would have some types flapping about in horror. Here again, it is important to realise that we are not all built the same way and that gentle coaxing is sometimes necessary to bring others round to your point of view. If you really have a fault it could be that you are so busy being your own, rather less than predictable self, that you fail to take the rest of the world into account.

# Taurus with Capricorn Ascendant

It might appear on the surface that you are not the most interesting person in the world. This is a pity, for you have an active though very logical mind, so logical in some instances that you would have a great deal in common with Mr Spock. This is the thorn in your flesh, or rather the flesh of everyone else, since you are probably quite happy being exactly what you are. You can think things through in a clear and very practical way and end up taking decisions that are balanced, eminently sensible, but, on occasions, rather dull.

Actually there is a fun machine somewhere deep within that Earth-sign nature and those who know you the best will recognise the fact. Often this combination is attended by a deep and biting sense of humour, but it's of the sort that less intelligent and considered types would find rather difficult to recognise. It is likely that you have no lack of confidence in your own judgement and you have all the attributes necessary to do very well on the financial front. Slow and steady progress is your way and you need to be quite certain before you commit yourself to any new venture. This is a zodiac combination that can soak up years of stress and numerous difficulties, yet still come out on top. Nothing holds you back for long and you tend to be very brave.

# Taurus with Aquarius Ascendant

There is nothing that you fail to think about deeply and with great intensity. You are wise, honest and very scientific in your approach to life. Routines are necessary in life, but you have most of them sorted out well in advance and so always have time to look at the next interesting fact. If you don't spend all your time watching documentaries on the television set, you make a good friend and love to socialise. Most of the great discoveries of the world were probably made by people with this sort of astrological combination, though your nature is rather 'odd' on occasions and so can be rather difficult for others to understand.

You may be most surprised when others tell you that you are eccentric, but you don't really mind too much because for half of the time you are not inhabiting the same world as the rest of us. Because you can be delightfully dotty you are probably much loved and cherished by your friends, of which there are likely to be many. Family members probably adore you too and you can be guaranteed to entertain anyone with whom you come into contact. The only fly in the ointment is that you sometimes lose track of reality, whatever that might be, and fly high in your own atmosphere of rarefied possibilities.

# Taurus with Pisces Ascendant

You are clearly a very sensitive type of person and that sometimes makes it rather difficult for others to know how they might best approach you. Private and deep, you are nevertheless socially inclined on many occasions. However, because your nature is bottomless it is possible that some types would actually accuse you of being shallow. How can this come about? Well, it's simple really. The fact is that you rarely show anyone what is going on in the deepest recesses of your mind and so your responses can appear to be trite or even ill-considered. This is far from the truth, as those who are allowed into the 'inner sanctum' would readily admit. You are something of a sensualist, and relish staying in bed late and simply pleasing yourself for days on end. However, you are a Taurean at heart so you desire a tidy environment in which to live your usually long life.

You are able to deal with the routine aspects of life quite well and can be a capable worker once you are up and firing on all cylinders. It is very important that you maintain an interest in what you are doing because the recesses of your dreamy mind can sometimes appear to be infinitely more attractive. Your imagination is second to none and this fact can often be turned to your advantage.

# Taurus with Aries Ascendant

This is a steady combination, so much so that even experienced astrologers would be unlikely to recognise that the Aries quality is present at all, unless of course they came to know you very well. Your approach to life tends to be slow and considered and there is a great danger that you could suppress those feelings that others of your kind would be only too willing to verbalise. To compensate, you are deeply creative and will think matters through much more readily than more dominant Aries types would be inclined to do. In your dealings with the world, you are, nevertheless, somewhat locked inside yourself and can struggle to achieve the level of communication that you so desperately need. Frustration might follow, were it not for the fact that you possess a quiet determination that, to those in the know, is the clearest window through to your Taurean soul.

The care for others is strong and you certainly demonstrate this at all levels. The fact is that you live a great percentage of your life in service to the people you take to, whilst at the same time being able to shut the door firmly in the face of people who irritate or anger you. You are deeply motivated towards family relationships.

# THE MOON AND THE PART IT PLAYS IN YOUR LIFE

In astrology the Moon is probably the single most important heavenly body after the Sun. Its unique position, as partner to the Earth on its journey around the solar system, means that the Moon appears to pass through the signs of the zodiac extremely quickly. The zodiac position of the Moon at the time of your birth plays a great part in personal character and is especially significant in the build-up of your emotional nature.

## Your Own Moon Sign

Discovering the position of the Moon at the time of your birth has always been notoriously difficult because tracking the complex zodiac positions of the Moon is not easy. This process has been reduced to three simple stages with our Lunar Tables. A breakdown of the Moon's zodiac positions can be found from page 35 onwards, so that once you know what your Moon Sign is, you can see what part this plays in the overall build-up of your personal character.

If you follow the instructions on the next page you will soon be able to work out exactly what zodiac sign the Moon occupied on the day that you were born and you can then go on to compare the reading for this position with those of your Sun sign and your Ascendant. It is partly the comparison between these three important positions that goes towards making you the unique individual you are.

# HOW TO DISCOVER YOUR MOON SIGN

This is a three-stage process. You may need a pen and a piece of paper but if you follow the instructions below the process should only take a minute or so.

**STAGE 1** First of all you need to know the Moon Age at the time of your birth. If you look at Moon Table 1, on page 33, you will find all the years between 1914 and 2012 down the left side. Find the year of your birth and then trace across to the right to the month of your birth. Where the two intersect you will find a number. This is the date of the New Moon in the month that you were born. You now need to count forward the number of days between the New Moon and your own birthday. For example, if the New Moon in the month of your birth was shown as being the 6th and you were born on the 20th, your Moon Age Day would be 14. If the New Moon in the month of your birth came after your birthday, you need to count forward from the New Moon in the previous month. Whatever the result, jot this number down so that you do not forget it.

**STAGE 2** Take a look at Moon Table 2 on page 34. Down the left hand column look for the date of your birth. Now trace across to the month of your birth. Where the two meet you will find a letter. Copy this letter down alongside your Moon Age Day.

**STAGE 3** Moon Table 3 on page 34 will supply you with the zodiac sign the Moon occupied on the day of your birth. Look for your Moon Age Day down the left hand column and then for the letter you found in Stage 2. Where the two converge you will find a zodiac sign and this is the sign occupied by the Moon on the day that you were born.

## Your Zodiac Moon Sign Explained

You will find a profile of all zodiac Moon Signs on pages 35 to 38, showing in yet another way how astrology helps to make you into the individual that you are. In each daily entry of the Astral Diary you can find the zodiac position of the Moon for every day of the year. This also allows you to discover your lunar birthdays. Since the Moon passes through all the signs of the zodiac in about a month, you can expect something like twelve lunar birthdays each year. At these times you are likely to be emotionally steady and able to make the sort of decisions that have real, lasting value.

## MOON TABLE 1

| YEAR | MAR | APR | MAY | YEAR | MAR | APR | MAY | YEAR | MAR | APR | MAY |
|------|-----|-----|-----|------|-----|-----|-----|------|-----|-----|-----|
| 1914 | 26 | 24 | 24 | 1947 | 21 | 20 | 19 | 1980 | 16 | 15 | 14 |
| 1915 | 15 | 13 | 13 | 1948 | 11 | 9 | 9 | 1981 | 6 | 4 | 4 |
| 1916 | 5 | 3 | 2 | 1949 | 29 | 28 | 27 | 1982 | 24 | 23 | 21 |
| 1917 | 23 | 22 | 20 | 1950 | 18 | 17 | 17 | 1983 | 14 | 13 | 12 |
| 1918 | 12 | 11 | 10 | 1951 | 7 | 6 | 6 | 1984 | 2 | 1 | 1/30 |
| 1919 | 2/31 | 30 | 29 | 1952 | 25 | 24 | 23 | 1985 | 21 | 20 | 19 |
| 1920 | 20 | 18 | 18 | 1953 | 15 | 13 | 13 | 1986 | 10 | 9 | 8 |
| 1921 | 9 | 8 | 7 | 1954 | 5 | 3 | 2 | 1987 | 29 | 28 | 27 |
| 1922 | 28 | 27 | 26 | 1955 | 24 | 22 | 21 | 1988 | 18 | 16 | 15 |
| 1923 | 17 | 16 | 15 | 1956 | 12 | 11 | 10 | 1989 | 7 | 6 | 5 |
| 1924 | 5 | 4 | 3 | 1957 | 1/31 | 29 | 29 | 1990 | 26 | 25 | 24 |
| 1925 | 24 | 23 | 22 | 1958 | 20 | 19 | 18 | 1991 | 15 | 13 | 13 |
| 1926 | 14 | 12 | 11 | 1959 | 9 | 8 | 7 | 1992 | 4 | 3 | 2 |
| 1927 | 3 | 2 | 1/30 | 1960 | 27 | 26 | 26 | 1993 | 24 | 22 | 21 |
| 1928 | 21 | 20 | 19 | 1961 | 16 | 15 | 14 | 1994 | 12 | 11 | 10 |
| 1929 | 11 | 9 | 9 | 1962 | 6 | 5 | 4 | 1995 | 30 | 29 | 29 |
| 1930 | 30 | 28 | 28 | 1963 | 25 | 23 | 23 | 1996 | 19 | 18 | 18 |
| 1931 | 19 | 18 | 17 | 1964 | 14 | 12 | 11 | 1997 | 9 | 7 | 6 |
| 1932 | 7 | 6 | 5 | 1965 | 2 | 1 | 1/30 | 1998 | 27 | 26 | 25 |
| 1933 | 26 | 24 | 24 | 1966 | 21 | 20 | 19 | 1999 | 17 | 16 | 15 |
| 1934 | 15 | 13 | 13 | 1967 | 10 | 9 | 8 | 2000 | 6 | 4 | 4 |
| 1935 | 5 | 3 | 2 | 1968 | 29 | 28 | 27 | 2001 | 24 | 23 | 22 |
| 1936 | 23 | 21 | 20 | 1969 | 18 | 16 | 15 | 2002 | 13 | 12 | 10 |
| 1937 | 13 | 12 | 10 | 1970 | 7 | 6 | 6 | 2003 | 2 | 1 | 1/30 |
| 1938 | 2/31 | 30 | 29 | 1971 | 26 | 25 | 24 | 2004 | 21 | 19 | 18 |
| 1939 | 20 | 19 | 19 | 1972 | 15 | 13 | 13 | 2005 | 10 | 8 | 8 |
| 1940 | 9 | 7 | 7 | 1973 | 5 | 3 | 2 | 2006 | 29 | 27 | 27 |
| 1941 | 27 | 26 | 26 | 1974 | 24 | 22 | 21 | 2007 | 18 | 17 | 15 |
| 1942 | 16 | 15 | 15 | 1975 | 12 | 11 | 11 | 2008 | 7 | 6 | 5 |
| 1943 | 6 | 4 | 4 | 1976 | 30 | 29 | 29 | 2009 | 26 | 25 | 24 |
| 1944 | 24 | 22 | 22 | 1977 | 19 | 18 | 18 | 2010 | 15 | 14 | 14 |
| 1945 | 14 | 12 | 11 | 1978 | 9 | 7 | 7 | 2011 | 5 | 3 | 3 |
| 1946 | 3 | 2 | 1/30 | 1979 | 27 | 26 | 26 | 2012 | 22 | 21 | 20 |

## TABLE 2

## MOON TABLE 3

| DAY | APR | MAY | M/D | J | K | L | M | N | O | P |
|-----|-----|-----|-----|-----|-----|-----|-----|-----|-----|-----|
| 1 | J | M | 0 | AR | TA | TA | TA | GE | GE | GE |
| 2 | J | M | 1 | TA | TA | TA | GE | GE | GE | CA |
| 3 | J | M | 2 | TA | TA | GE | GE | GE | CA | CA |
| 4 | J | M | 3 | TA | GE | GE | GE | CA | CA | CA |
| 5 | J | M | 4 | GE | GE | GE | CA | CA | CA | LE |
| 6 | J | M | 5 | GE | CA | CA | CA | LE | LE | LE |
| 7 | J | M | 6 | CA | CA | CA | LE | LE | LE | VI |
| 8 | J | M | 7 | CA | CA | LE | LE | LE | VI | VI |
| 9 | J | M | 8 | CA | LE | LE | LE | VI | VI | VI |
| 10 | J | M | 9 | LE | LE | VI | VI | VI | LI | LI |
| 11 | K | M | 10 | LE | VI | VI | VI | LI | LI | LI |
| 12 | K | N | 11 | VI | VI | VI | LI | LI | SC | SC |
| 13 | K | N | 12 | VI | VI | LI | LI | LI | SC | SC |
| 14 | K | N | 13 | VI | LI | LI | LI | SC | SC | SC |
| 15 | K | N | 14 | LI | LI | LI | SC | SC | SA | SA |
| 16 | K | N | 15 | LI | SC | SC | SC | SA | SA | SA |
| 17 | K | N | 16 | SC | SC | SC | SA | SA | SA | CP |
| 18 | K | N | 17 | SC | SC | SA | SA | SA | CP | CP |
| 19 | K | N | 18 | SC | SA | SA | SA | CP | CP | CP |
| 20 | K | N | 19 | SA | SA | SA | CP | CP | CP | AQ |
| 21 | L | N | 20 | SA | CP | CP | CP | AQ | AQ | AQ |
| 22 | L | O | 21 | CP | CP | CP | AQ | AQ | AQ | PI |
| 23 | L | O | 22 | CP | CP | AQ | AQ | AQ | PI | PI |
| 24 | L | O | 23 | CP | AQ | AQ | AQ | PI | PI | PI |
| 25 | L | O | 24 | AQ | AQ | AQ | PI | PI | PI | AR |
| 26 | L | O | 25 | AQ | PI | PI | PI | AR | AR | AR |
| 27 | L | O | 26 | PI | PI | PI | AR | AR | AR | TA |
| 28 | L | O | 27 | PI | PI | AR | AR | AR | TA | TA |
| 29 | L | O | 28 | PI | AR | AR | AR | TA | TA | TA |
| 30 | L | O | 29 | AR | AR | AR | TA | TA | TA | GE |
| 31 | – | O | | | | | | | | |

AR = Aries, TA = Taurus, GE = Gemini, CA = Cancer, LE = Leo, VI = Virgo,
LI = Libra, SC = Scorpio, SA = Sagittarius, CP = Capricorn, AQ = Aquarius, PI = Pisces

# MOON SIGNS

## Moon in Aries

You have a strong imagination, courage, determination and a desire to do things in your own way and forge your own path through life.

Originality is a key attribute; you are seldom stuck for ideas although your mind is changeable and you could take the time to focus on individual tasks. Often quick-tempered, you take orders from few people and live life at a fast pace. Avoid health problems by taking regular time out for rest and relaxation.

Emotionally, it is important that you talk to those you are closest to and work out your true feelings. Once you discover that people are there to help, there is less necessity for you to do everything yourself.

## Moon in Taurus

The Moon in Taurus gives you a courteous and friendly manner, which means you are likely to have many friends.

The good things in life mean a lot to you, as Taurus is an Earth sign that delights in experiences which please the senses. Hence you are probably a lover of good food and drink, which may in turn mean you need to keep an eye on the bathroom scales, especially as looking good is also important to you.

Emotionally you are fairly stable and you stick by your own standards. Taureans do not respond well to change. Intuition also plays an important part in your life.

## Moon in Gemini

You have a warm-hearted character, sympathetic and eager to help others. At times reserved, you can also be articulate and chatty: this is part of the paradox of Gemini, which always brings duplicity to the nature. You are interested in current affairs, have a good intellect, and are good company and likely to have many friends. Most of your friends have a high opinion of you and would be ready to defend you should the need arise. However, this is usually unnecessary, as you are quite capable of defending yourself in any verbal confrontation.

Travel is important to your inquisitive mind and you find intellectual stimulus in mixing with people from different cultures. You also gain much from reading, writing and the arts but you do need plenty of rest and relaxation in order to avoid fatigue.

## Moon in Cancer

The Moon in Cancer at the time of birth is a fortunate position as Cancer is the Moon's natural home. This means that the qualities of compassion and understanding given by the Moon are especially enhanced in your nature, and you are friendly and sociable and cope well with emotional pressures. You cherish home and family life, and happily do the domestic tasks. Your surroundings are important to you and you hate squalor and filth. You are likely to have a love of music and poetry.

Your basic character, although at times changeable like the Moon itself, depends on symmetry. You aim to make your surroundings comfortable and harmonious, for yourself and those close to you.

## Moon in Leo

The best qualities of the Moon and Leo come together to make you warm-hearted, fair, ambitious and self-confident. With good organisational abilities, you invariably rise to a position of responsibility in your chosen career. This is fortunate as you don't enjoy being an 'also-ran' and would rather be an important part of a small organisation than a menial in a large one.

You should be lucky in love, and happy, provided you put in the effort to make a comfortable home for yourself and those close to you. It is likely that you will have a love of pleasure, sport, music and literature. Life brings you many rewards, most of them as a direct result of your own efforts, although you may be luckier than average and ready to make the best of any situation.

## Moon in Virgo

You are endowed with good mental abilities and a keen receptive memory, but you are never ostentatious or pretentious. Naturally quite reserved, you still have many friends, especially of the opposite sex. Marital relationships must be discussed carefully and worked at so that they remain harmonious, as personal attachments can be a problem if you do not give them your full attention.

Talented and persevering, you possess artistic qualities and are a good homemaker. Earning your honours through genuine merit, you work long and hard towards your objectives but show little pride in your achievements. Many short journeys will be undertaken in your life.

# Moon in Libra

With the Moon in Libra you are naturally popular and make friends easily. People like you, probably more than you realise, you bring fun to a party and are a natural diplomat. For all its good points, Libra is not the most stable of astrological signs and, as a result, your emotions can be a little unstable too. Therefore, although the Moon in Libra is said to be good for love and marriage, your Sun sign and Rising sign will have an important effect on your emotional and loving qualities.

You must remember to relate to others in your decision-making. Co-operation is crucial because Libra represents the 'balance' of life that can only be achieved through harmonious relationships. Conformity is not easy for you because Libra, an Air sign, likes its independence.

# Moon in Scorpio

Some people might call you pushy. In fact, all you really want to do is to live life to the full and protect yourself and your family from the pressures of life. Take care to avoid giving the impression of being sarcastic or impulsive and use your energies wisely and constructively.

You have great courage and you invariably achieve your goals by force of personality and sheer effort. You are fond of mystery and are good at predicting the outcome of situations and events. Travel experiences can be beneficial to you.

You may experience problems if you do not take time to examine your motives in a relationship, and also if you allow jealousy, always a feature of Scorpio, to cloud your judgement.

# Moon in Sagittarius

The Moon in Sagittarius helps to make you a generous individual with humanitarian qualities and a kind heart. Restlessness may be intrinsic as your mind is seldom still. Perhaps because of this, you have a need for change that could lead you to several major moves during your adult life. You are not afraid to stand your ground when you know your judgement is right, you speak directly and have good intuition.

At work you are quick, efficient and versatile and so you make an ideal employee. You need work to be intellectually demanding and do not enjoy tedious routines.

In relationships, you anger quickly if faced with stupidity or deception, though you are just as quick to forgive and forget. Emotionally, there are times when your heart rules your head.

## Moon in Capricorn

The Moon in Capricorn makes you popular and likely to come into the public eye in some way. The watery Moon is not entirely comfortable in the Earth sign of Capricorn and this may lead to some difficulties in the early years of life. An initial lack of creative ability and indecision must be overcome before the true qualities of patience and perseverance inherent in Capricorn can show through.

You have good administrative ability and are a capable worker, and if you are careful you can accumulate wealth. But you must be cautious and take professional advice in partnerships, as you are open to deception. You may be interested in social or welfare work, which suit your organisational skills and sympathy for others.

## Moon in Aquarius

The Moon in Aquarius makes you an active and agreeable person with a friendly, easy-going nature. Sympathetic to the needs of others, you flourish in a laid-back atmosphere. You are broad-minded, fair and open to suggestion, although sometimes you have an unconventional quality which others can find hard to understand.

You are interested in the strange and curious, and in old articles and places. You enjoy trips to these places and gain much from them. Political, scientific and educational work interests you and you might choose a career in science or technology.

Money-wise, you make gains through innovation and concentration and Lunar Aquarians often tackle more than one job at a time. In love you are kind and honest.

## Moon in Pisces

You have a kind, sympathetic nature, somewhat retiring at times, but you always take account of others' feelings and help when you can.

Personal relationships may be problematic, but as life goes on you can learn from your experiences and develop a better understanding of yourself and the world around you.

You have a fondness for travel, appreciate beauty and harmony and hate disorder and strife. You may be fond of literature and would make a good writer or speaker yourself. You have a creative imagination and may come across as an incurable romantic. You have strong intuition, maybe bordering on a mediumistic quality, which sets you apart from the mass. You may not be rich in cash terms, but your personal gifts are worth more than gold.

# TAURUS IN LOVE

Discover how compatible in love you are with people from the same and other signs of the zodiac. Five stars equals a match made in heaven!

## Taurus meets Taurus

A certainty for complete success or absolute failure. Taurus has enough self-knowledge to recognise the strengths of a fellow Taurean, so these two can live in harmony. Both will be tidy and live in comfortable surroundings. Two Taureans seldom argue and will be good friends. But something may be lacking – a spark that doesn't ignite. Passion is important and Taurus reflects, rather than creates it. The prognosis is good, but someone must turn the heat up to get things really cooking. Star rating: ****

## Taurus meets Gemini

Gemini people can infuriate the generally steady Taurean nature as they are so untidy, which is a complete reversal of the Taurean ethos. At first this won't matter; Mr or Miss Gemini is enchanting, entertaining and very different. But time will tell, and that's why this potential relationship only has two stars. There is hope, however, because Taurus can curb some of the excesses of the Twins, whilst Gemini is capable of preventing the Bull from taking itself too seriously. Star rating: **

## Taurus meets Cancer

This pair will have the tidiest house in the street – every stick of furniture in place, and no errant blade of grass daring to spoil the lawn. But things inside the relationship might not be quite so ship-shape as both signs need, but don't offer, encouragement. There's plenty of affection, but few incentives for mutual progress. This might not prevent material success, but an enduring relationship isn't based on money alone. Passion is essential, and both parties need to realise and aim for that. Star rating: **

## Taurus meets Leo

Here we find a generally successful pairing, which frequently leads to an enduring relationship. Taurus needs stimulation which Leo is happy to offer, while Leo responds well to the Bull's sense of order. The essence of the relationship is balance, but it may be achieved with wild swings of the scales on the way, so don't expect a quiet life, though this pair will enjoy a reconciliation after an argument! Material success is probable and, as both like children, a family is likely. Star rating: ***

## Taurus meets Virgo

This is a difficult basis for a successful relationship, and yet it often works. Both signs are from the Earth element, so have a common-sense approach to life. They have a mutual understanding, and share many interests. Taurus understands and copes well with Virgo's fussy nature, while Virgo revels in the Bull's tidy and artistic qualities. Both sides are committed to achieving lasting material success. There won't be fireworks, and the match may lack a certain 'spiritual' feel, but as that works both ways it may not be a problem. Star rating: *****

## Taurus meets Libra

A happy life is important to both these signs and, as they are both ruled by Venus, they share a common understanding, even though they display themselves so differently. Taurus is quieter than Libra, but can be decisive, and that's what counts. Libra is interested in absolutely everything, an infectious quality when seen through Taurean eyes. The slightly flighty qualities of Libra may lead to jealousy from the Bull. Not an argumentative relationship and one that often works well. There could be many changes of address for this pair. Star rating: ****

## Taurus meets Scorpio

Scorpio is deep – very deep – which may be a problem, because Taurus doesn't wear its heart on its sleeve either. It might be difficult for this pair to get together, because neither are naturally inclined to make the first move. Taurus stands in awe of the power and intensity of the Scorpio mind, while the Scorpion is interested in the Bull's affable and friendly qualities, so an enduring relationship could be forged if the couple ever get round to talking. Both are lovers of home and family, which will help to cement a relationship. Star rating: **

## Taurus meets Sagittarius

On first impression, Taurus may not like Sagittarius, who may seem brash, and even common, when viewed through the Bull's refined eyes. But there is hope of success because the two signs have so much to offer each other. The Archer is enthralled by the Taurean's natural poise and beauty, while Taurus always needs more basic confidence, which is no problem to Sagittarius who has plenty to spare. Both signs love to travel. There are certain to be ups and downs, but that doesn't prevent an interesting, inspiring and even exciting combination. Star rating: ***

## Taurus meets Capricorn

If not quite a match made in heaven, this comes close. Both signs are earthy in nature and that is a promising start. Capricorn is very practical and can make a Taurean's dreams come true. Both are tidy, like to know what is going to happen in a day-to-day sense, and are steady and committed. Taurus loves refinement, which Capricorn accepts and even helps to create. A good prognosis for material success rounds off a relationship that could easily stay the course. The only thing missing is a genuine sense of humour. Star rating: *****

## Taurus meets Aquarius

In any relationship of which Aquarius is a part, surprises abound. It is difficult for Taurus to understand the soul-searching, adventurous, changeable Aquarian, but on the positive side, the Bull is adaptable and can respond well to a dose of excitement. Aquarians are kind and react well to the same quality coming back at them. Both are friendly, capable of deep affection and basically quite creative. Unfortunately, though, Taurus simply doesn't know what makes Aquarius tick, which could lead to hidden feelings of isolation. Star rating: **

## Taurus meets Pisces

No problem here, unless both parties come from the quieter side of their respective signs. Most of the time Taurus and Pisces would live comfortably together, offering mutual support and deep regard. Taurus can offer the personal qualities that Pisces craves, whilst Pisces understands and copes with the Bull's slightly stubborn qualities. Taurus is likely to travel in Piscean company, so there is a potential for wide-ranging experiences and variety which is essential. There will be some misunderstandings, mainly because Pisces is so deep, but that won't prevent their enduring happiness. Star rating: ***

## Taurus meets Aries

This match has been known to work very well. Aries brings dynamism and ambition, while Taurus has the patience to see things through logically. Such complementary views work equally well in a relationship or in an office environment. There is mutual respect, but sometimes a lack of total understanding. The romantic needs of each sign are quite different, but both are still fulfilled. Taurus and Aries can live easily in domestic harmony which is very important but, interestingly, Aries may be the loser in battles of will. Star rating: ***

# VENUS:
# THE PLANET OF LOVE

If you look up at the sky around sunset or sunrise you will often see Venus in close attendance to the Sun. It is arguably one of the most beautiful sights of all and there is little wonder that historically it became associated with the goddess of love. But although Venus does play an important part in the way you view love and in the way others see you romantically, this is only one of the spheres of influence that it enjoys in your overall character.

Venus has a part to play in the more cultured side of your life and has much to do with your appreciation of art, literature, music and general creativity. Even the way you look is responsive to the part of the zodiac that Venus occupied at the start of your life, though this fact is also down to your Sun sign and Ascending sign. If, at the time you were born, Venus occupied one of the more gregarious zodiac signs, you will be more likely to wear your heart on your sleeve, as well as to be more attracted to entertainment, social gatherings and good company. If on the other hand Venus occupied a quiet zodiac sign at the time of your birth, you would tend to be more retiring and less willing to shine in public situations.

It's good to know what part the planet Venus plays in your life, for it can have a great bearing on the way you appear to the rest of the world and since we all have to mix with others, you can learn to make the very best of what Venus has to offer you.

One of the great complications in the past has always been trying to establish exactly what zodiac position Venus enjoyed when you were born, because the planet is notoriously difficult to track. However, we have solved that problem by creating a table that is exclusive to your Sun sign, which you will find on the following page.

Establishing your Venus sign could not be easier. Just look up the year of your birth on the following page and you will see a sign of the zodiac. This was the sign that Venus occupied in the period covered by your sign in that year. If Venus occupied more than one sign during the period, this is indicated by the date on which the sign changed, and the name of the new sign. For instance, if you were born in 1950, Venus was in Pisces until the 5th May, after which time it was in Aries. If you were born before 5th May your Venus sign is Pisces, if you were born on or after 5th May, your Venus sign is Aries. Once you have established the position of Venus at the time of your birth, you can then look in the pages which follow to see how this has a bearing on your life as a whole.

1914 TAURUS / 2.5 GEMINI
1915 PISCES / 27.4 ARIES
1916 GEMINI / 6.5 CANCER
1917 TAURUS / 16.5 GEMINI
1918 PISCES / 7.5 ARIES
1919 GEMINI / 13.5 CANCER
1920 ARIES / 7.5 TAURUS
1921 TAURUS / 27.4 ARIES
1922 TAURUS / 2.5 GEMINI
1923 PISCES / 27.4 ARIES
1924 GEMINI / 7.5 CANCER
1925 TAURUS / 16.5 GEMINI
1926 PISCES / 6.5 ARIES
1927 GEMINI / 12.5 CANCER
1928 ARIES / 6.5 TAURUS
1929 TAURUS / 24.4 ARIES
1930 TAURUS / 1.5 GEMINI
1931 PISCES / 26.4 ARIES
1932 GEMINI / 8.5 CANCER
1933 TAURUS / 15.5 GEMINI
1934 PISCES / 6.5 ARIES
1935 GEMINI / 12.5 CANCER
1936 ARIES / 6.5 TAURUS
1937 TAURUS / 21.4 ARIES
1938 TAURUS / 1.5 GEMINI
1939 PISCES / 26.4 ARIES
1940 GEMINI / 9.5 CANCER
1941 TAURUS / 14.5 GEMINI
1942 PISCES / 6.5 ARIES
1943 GEMINI / 11.5 CANCER
1944 ARIES / 6.5 TAURUS
1945 ARIES
1946 TAURUS / 30.4 GEMINI
1947 PISCES / 25.4 ARIES
1948 GEMINI / 9.5 CANCER
1949 TAURUS / 14.5 GEMINI
1950 PISCES / 5.5 ARIES
1951 GEMINI / 11.5 CANCER
1952 ARIES / 5.5 TAURUS
1953 ARIES
1954 TAURUS / 29.4 GEMINI
1955 PISCES / 25.4 ARIES
1956 GEMINI / 10.5 CANCER
1957 TAURUS / 13.5 GEMINI
1958 PISCES / 5.5 ARIES
1959 GEMINI / 10.5 CANCER
1960 ARIES / 4.5 TAURUS
1961 ARIES
1962 TAURUS / 28.4 GEMINI
1963 PISCES / 24.4 ARIES

1964 GEMINI / 11.5 CANCER
1965 TAURUS / 13.5 GEMINI
1966 PISCES / 5.5 ARIES
1967 GEMINI / 10.5 CANCER
1968 ARIES / 4.5 TAURUS
1969 ARIES
1970 TAURUS / 27.4 GEMINI
1971 PISCES / 24.4 ARIES
1972 GEMINI / 12.5 CANCER
1973 TAURUS / 12.5 GEMINI
1974 PISCES / 4.5 ARIES
1975 GEMINI / 9.5 CANCER
1976 ARIES / 3.5 TAURUS
1977 ARIES
1978 TAURUS / 27.4 GEMINI
1979 PISCES / 23.4 ARIES
1980 GEMINI / 13.5 CANCER
1981 TAURUS / 12.5 GEMINI
1982 PISCES / 4.5 ARIES
1983 GEMINI / 9.5 CANCER
1984 ARIES / 3.5 TAURUS
1985 ARIES
1986 TAURUS / 26.4 GEMINI
1987 PISCES / 23.4 ARIES
1988 GEMINI / 15.5 CANCER
1989 TAURUS / 11.5 GEMINI
1990 PISCES / 4.5 ARIES
1991 GEMINI / 8.5 CANCER
1992 ARIES / 2.5 TAURUS
1993 ARIES
1994 TAURUS / 26.4 GEMINI
1995 PISCES / 22.4 ARIES
1996 GEMINI / 15.5 CANCER
1997 TAURUS / 11.5 GEMINI
1998 PISCES / 3.5 ARIES
1999 GEMINI / 8.5 CANCER
2000 ARIES / 2.5 TAURUS
2001 ARIES
2002 TAURUS / 26.4 GEMINI
2003 PISCES / 22.4 ARIES
2004 GEMINI / 15.5 CANCER
2005 TAURUS / 11.5 GEMINI
2006 PISCES / 3.5 ARIES
2007 GEMINI / 8.5 CANCER
2008 ARIES / 2.5 TAURUS
2009 ARIES
2010 TAURUS / 26.4 GEMINI
2011 PISCES / 22.4 ARIES
2012 PISCES / 22.4 ARIES

# VENUS THROUGH THE ZODIAC SIGNS

## Venus in Aries

Amongst other things, the position of Venus in Aries indicates a fondness for travel, music and all creative pursuits. Your nature tends to be affectionate and you would try not to create confusion or difficulty for others if it could be avoided. Many people with this planetary position have a great love of the theatre, and mental stimulation is of the greatest importance. Early romantic attachments are common with Venus in Aries, so it is very important to establish a genuine sense of romantic continuity. Early marriage is not recommended, especially if it is based on sympathy. You may give your heart a little too readily on occasions.

## Venus in Taurus

You are capable of very deep feelings and your emotions tend to last for a very long time. This makes you a trusting partner and lover, whose constancy is second to none. In life you are precise and careful and always try to do things the right way. Although this means an ordered life, which you are comfortable with, it can also lead you to be rather too fussy for your own good. Despite your pleasant nature, you are very fixed in your opinions and quite able to speak your mind. Others are attracted to you and historical astrologers always quoted this position of Venus as being very fortunate in terms of marriage. However, if you find yourself involved in a failed relationship, it could take you a long time to trust again.

## Venus in Gemini

As with all associations related to Gemini, you tend to be quite versatile, anxious for change and intelligent in your dealings with the world at large. You may gain money from more than one source but you are equally good at spending it. There is an inference here that you are a good communicator, via either the written or the spoken word, and you love to be in the company of interesting people. Always on the look-out for culture, you may also be very fond of music, and love to indulge the curious and cultured side of your nature. In romance you tend to have more than one relationship and could find yourself associated with someone who has previously been a friend or even a distant relative.

## Venus in Cancer

You often stay close to home because you are very fond of family and enjoy many of your most treasured moments when you are with those you love. Being naturally sympathetic, you will always do anything you can to support those around you, even people you hardly know at all. This charitable side of your nature is your most noticeable trait and is one of the reasons why others are naturally so fond of you. Being receptive and in some cases even psychic, you can see through to the soul of most of those with whom you come into contact. You may not commence too many romantic attachments but when you do give your heart, it tends to be unconditionally.

## Venus in Leo

It must become quickly obvious to almost anyone you meet that you are kind, sympathetic and yet determined enough to stand up for anyone or anything that is truly important to you. Bright and sunny, you warm the world with your natural enthusiasm and would rarely do anything to hurt those around you, or at least not intentionally. In romance you are ardent and sincere, though some may find your style just a little overpowering. Gains come through your contacts with other people and this could be especially true with regard to romance, for love and money often come hand in hand for those who were born with Venus in Leo. People claim to understand you, though you are more complex than you seem.

## Venus in Virgo

Your nature could well be fairly quiet no matter what your Sun sign might be, though this fact often manifests itself as an inner peace and would not prevent you from being basically sociable. Some delays and even the odd disappointment in love cannot be ruled out with this planetary position, though it's a fact that you will usually find the happiness you look for in the end. Catapulting yourself into romantic entanglements that you know to be rather ill-advised is not sensible, and it would be better to wait before you committed yourself exclusively to any one person. It is the essence of your nature to serve the world at large and through doing so it is possible that you will attract money at some stage in your life.

## Venus in Libra

Venus is very comfortable in Libra and bestows upon those people who have this planetary position a particular sort of kindness that is easy to recognise. This is a very good position for all sorts of friendships and also for romantic attachments that usually bring much joy into your life. Few individuals with Venus in Libra would avoid marriage and since you are capable of great depths of love, it is likely that you will find a contented personal life. You like to mix with people of integrity and intelligence but don't take kindly to scruffy surroundings or work that means getting your hands too dirty. Careful speculation, good business dealings and money through marriage all seem fairly likely.

## Venus in Scorpio

You are quite open and tend to spend money quite freely, even on those occasions when you don't have very much. Although your intentions are always good, there are times when you get yourself in to the odd scrape and this can be particularly true when it comes to romance, which you may come to late or from a rather unexpected direction. Certainly you have the power to be happy and to make others contented on the way, but you find the odd stumbling block on your journey through life and it could seem that you have to work harder than those around you. As a result of this, you gain a much deeper understanding of the true value of personal happiness than many people ever do, and are likely to achieve true contentment in the end.

## Venus in Sagittarius

You are lighthearted, cheerful and always able to see the funny side of any situation. These facts enhance your popularity, which is especially high with members of the opposite sex. You should never have to look too far to find romantic interest in your life, though it is just possible that you might be too willing to commit yourself before you are certain that the person in question is right for you. Part of the problem here extends to other areas of life too. The fact is that you like variety in everything and so can tire of situations that fail to offer it. All the same, if you choose wisely and learn to understand your restless side, then great happiness can be yours.

## Venus in Capricorn

The most notable trait that comes from Venus in this position is that it makes you trustworthy and able to take on all sorts of responsibilities in life. People are instinctively fond of you and love you all the more because you are always ready to help those who are in any form of need. Social and business popularity can be yours and there is a magnetic quality to your nature that is particularly attractive in a romantic sense. Anyone who wants a partner for a lover, a spouse and a good friend too would almost certainly look in your direction. Constancy is the hallmark of your nature and unfaithfulness would go right against the grain. You might sometimes be a little too trusting.

## Venus in Aquarius

This location of Venus offers a fondness for travel and a desire to try out something new at every possible opportunity. You are extremely easy to get along with and tend to have many friends from varied backgrounds, classes and inclinations. You like to live a distinct sort of life and gain a great deal from moving about, both in a career sense and with regard to your home. It is not out of the question that you could form a romantic attachment to someone who comes from far away or be attracted to a person of a distinctly artistic and original nature. What you cannot stand is jealousy, for you have friends of both sexes and would want to keep things that way.

## Venus in Pisces

The first thing people tend to notice about you is your wonderful, warm smile. Being very charitable by nature you will do anything to help others, even if you don't know them well. Much of your life may be spent sorting out situations for other people, but it is very important to feel that you are living for yourself too. In the main, you remain cheerful, and tend to be quite attractive to members of the opposite sex. Where romantic attachments are concerned, you could be drawn to people who are significantly older or younger than yourself or to someone with a unique career or point of view. It might be best for you to avoid marrying whilst you are still very young.

# TAURUS:
# 2011 DIARY PAGES

# October

2011

## 1 SATURDAY
*Moon Age Day 4    Moon Sign Scorpio*

The first day of October may not be the most advantageous for you, though it should have less of a bearing on your working life since it arrives at the weekend. The lunar low can still cause you one or two problems, mostly in terms of the way you communicate with others, but you have scope to look towards greater achievements later.

## 2 SUNDAY
*Moon Age Day 5    Moon Sign Sagittarius*

Make the most of a great resurgence of determination and prove that you can't keep a good Taurus subject down for long. When it comes to achieving your objectives you can now be second to none, and you might even be able to turn this into one of the most important Sundays of the year. Just keep facing your ultimate goals.

## 3 MONDAY
*Moon Age Day 6    Moon Sign Sagittarius*

Keeping busy is the name of the game today, and it's all about making the best out of almost any sort of circumstance. Watch out for the odd minor mishap, possibly brought about as a result of carelessness exhibited by someone else. You can use your present quick thinking to show that you are good to have around in any tight corner.

## 4 TUESDAY
*Moon Age Day 7    Moon Sign Sagittarius*

There is no reason whatsoever to hang back at the moment, even if things turn out to be slightly different for the rest of the working week. If there is anything that needs doing, and that requires large amounts of energy, today is the ideal day to tackle it. It's natural to feel tired after such exertions, but that needn't stop you socialising!

# 5 WEDNESDAY
*Moon Age Day 8    Moon Sign Capricorn*

The practical world is still doing you the odd favour, allowing you to make gains, particularly in a financial sense. Rules and regulations shouldn't be too difficult to follow now, and you should be willing to conform when it is necessary. Be prepared to help friends who have specific problems, and also be supportive of family members.

# 6 THURSDAY
*Moon Age Day 9    Moon Sign Capricorn*

An ideal time to put the pursuit of wealth on your list of priorities. Taurus may not be the most acquisitive of the zodiac signs, but it isn't too far behind. It's all down to a sense of security, which Taurus usually desires. Casting your mind forward, you now have scope to do some deals that will feather your nest in the days and weeks ahead.

# 7 FRIDAY
*Moon Age Day 10    Moon Sign Aquarius*

There are signs that love is mainly where your interests should be centred on this October Friday. It's about relishing the company of someone who cares about you deeply, and doing something in return. In more casual attachments, be prepared to deal with the confusing attitudes of others, especially if they won't take advice.

# 8 SATURDAY
*Moon Age Day 11    Moon Sign Aquarius*

Compromise is your middle name today, or at least it if isn't, then it should be. You can get more today by being willing to give a little than at just about any other time this month. Some nostalgia is possible, but that is part of the way present trends make themselves felt in your life. By tomorrow you should be flying high again.

# 9 SUNDAY
*Moon Age Day 12    Moon Sign Aquarius*

You have what it takes to attract a great deal of positive attention around this time. This is the case in both a personal and a more general sense. Popularity is everything to you now, and you needn't hold back in terms of the love you offer in return. Almost anyone could feel your warmth during most of this month.

# 10 MONDAY
*Moon Age Day 13   Moon Sign Pisces*

A boost is on offer for work developments and this ought to be a good time for firming up some of your plans for the immediate and longer-term future. Make the most of any ingenious way you can devise for getting ahead in a professional sense, and don't be afraid to latch on to anything you see as being advantageous.

# 11 TUESDAY
*Moon Age Day 14   Moon Sign Pisces*

Trends indicate a slight sense of social reluctance today. This is down to the influence of the Moon moving into your solar twelfth house, which often offers scope for a quieter interlude and for some necessary introspection on your part. In two or three days all opportunities open up for you again, but for the moment, why not take a break?

# 12 WEDNESDAY
*Moon Age Day 15   Moon Sign Aries*

It shouldn't be difficult for you to work with people in authority at the moment. Now is the time to show how compliant and willing to co-operate you can be, particularly when you consider that the suggestions being made are sensible. Irritations are possible, but these may be linked to determination on your part that cannot be utilised yet.

# 13 THURSDAY
*Moon Age Day 16   Moon Sign Aries*

By tomorrow you can ensure that the complexion of your life looks rather different than it does at the moment. If today seems to offer little in the way of forward movement, there's nothing to prevent you from planning your future moves. Be content to allow a little time to pass, and watch for opportunities you can utilise tomorrow.

# 14 FRIDAY
*Moon Age Day 17   Moon Sign Taurus*

Now the lunar high is with you again, making this an ideal time to think up plenty of new and potentially great schemes. It's time to show how active and enterprising you can be, and you have everything you need to get on board with people who are already motoring. A combination of enterprise and co-operation can work wonders.

# 15 SATURDAY
*Moon Age Day 18   Moon Sign Taurus*

A lucky spell is on offer, so this would be a good day to make an early start and to capitalise on the opportunities that stand around you. Keep abreast of news and views in your working environment and also make the best of new social opportunities that you can identify around this time. Your confidence level is enhanced at present.

# 16 SUNDAY
*Moon Age Day 19   Moon Sign Gemini*

You have scope to make this a very busy day, even if you are not committed to working. There are gains to be made in your financial dealings, and it is also a chance to get more in tune with any family members who have caused you problems recently. Rather than waiting to be asked in any situation that appeals to you – go for it!

# 17 MONDAY
*Moon Age Day 20   Moon Sign Gemini*

Prepare to demonstrate your pleasing manner when it comes to self-expression, as well as your ability to win over other people, even those who can sometimes prove to be difficult. Such are your powers of communication that you can make a great impression on the world at every level, and your charms ensure that everyone wants to know you.

# 18 TUESDAY
*Moon Age Day 21   Moon Sign Gemini*

You can get even more from being on the go today. The Moon is in a favourable position for you and it can be especially helpful when it comes to expressing your emotions. This would be an excellent time for a heart-to-heart with your lover, and you are in a good position to think up the sort of compliments that make a difference.

# 19 WEDNESDAY
*Moon Age Day 22   Moon Sign Cancer*

Affairs of the heart are still well accented for you, and there are potential gains to be made from forming new attachments or stepping up the social pressure once work is out of the way. The middle of this week might be especially useful for starting new projects that are of no practical benefit, but are potentially enjoyable.

## 20 THURSDAY
*Moon Age Day 23    Moon Sign Cancer*

A boost to all communication issues is now on offer, and with Mercury now in your solar seventh house it's worth your while listening to everything that the jungle drums are saying. There are times when you may put two and two together, only to make five, but on the whole you remain fairly astute and are not easily fooled.

## 21 FRIDAY
*Moon Age Day 24    Moon Sign Leo*

As far as your career is concerned your best approach today is to go it alone to a greater extent than would normally be the case. This is particularly appropriate if either you can't find the advice you need or else colleagues do not seem quite as reliable as you wish. Taurus can be very single-minded, and this could well be the case around now.

## 22 SATURDAY
*Moon Age Day 25    Moon Sign Leo*

Domestic matters could bring problems, particularly those inspired by clashes of will and by a continued tendency on your part to expect rather than to know. Be prepared to check on the way others are feeling before you put your own plans into action. Once you are fully in the know it should be easier to make the right decisions.

## 23 SUNDAY
*Moon Age Day 26    Moon Sign Virgo*

This is a day that is all about getting yourself noticed. In fact, there's nothing wrong with setting out your stall specifically to make sure that you are. It's a question of looking your best and attracting the sort of people you find fascinating. Present trends can enhance the appeal of Taurus, so make sure this is obvious to others.

## 24 MONDAY
*Moon Age Day 27    Moon Sign Virgo*

Don't be afraid to put forward your intuitive ideas for discussion readily. You have what it takes to convince others to take your opinions on board, and can attract a broad spectrum of assistance for your plans. Even if getting exactly what you want isn't very easy, being the sort of person you are, you needn't settle for second-best.

## 25 TUESDAY          *Moon Age Day 28    Moon Sign Libra*

Socially speaking you should now definitely be on the up again.
Relationships offer everything you might hope for and can certainly
help you to bring out the best in yourself. Confidence ought to
remain fairly high, even though there may be a slight downward
turn towards the end of the week. Keep repeating things you know
to be true.

## 26 WEDNESDAY          *Moon Age Day 29    Moon Sign Libra*

This will be one of the main days of the week for busy preparations
and for making sure that everything you need is in place for your plans
to mature later. Current trends assist you to work on several different
fronts at the same time, though you could well find yourself running
out of steam if you also go for a very hectic social time this evening.

## 27 THURSDAY          *Moon Age Day 0    Moon Sign Scorpio*

The arrival of the lunar low encourages you to put the brakes on as
far as some of your more practical efforts are concerned, and under
this influence a slower and steadier approach is your best option.
Don't be afraid to seek advice from people in the know. It's also
important to make sure you have sufficient time to listen to them!

## 28 FRIDAY          *Moon Age Day 1    Moon Sign Scorpio*

Even if progress in your daily life remains generally slow, that doesn't
mean you can't make any headway at all. Prior planning is the order
of the day, together with getting little details sorted out that will
make your path easier in a day or two. However, as far as genuine,
practical movement is concerned, being patient is the key.

## 29 SATURDAY          *Moon Age Day 2    Moon Sign Sagittarius*

Getting yourself in people's good books today can assist you to
make gains you probably didn't expect. Coming out of the lunar
low can be a little like being shot out of a cannon, so you need to
be aware that some aspects of today are going to be fast and furious.
New activities are in the offing, so look at the potential carefully.

# 30 SUNDAY    *Moon Age Day 3    Moon Sign Sagittarius*

Today has potential to be quite light-hearted and demands a very gentle touch. Any tendency to get too serious about things may not meet with a positive response from others, so you need to show just how humorous and jolly you are capable of being. This is especially necessary in personal attachments and with regard to romance.

# 31 MONDAY    *Moon Age Day 4    Moon Sign Capricorn*

Social get-togethers are a good way to start the week, even if these have to be arranged at the last minute because you are busy at work. You also have scope to mix business with pleasure to a great extent, and there's nothing wrong with having the end of the year in your sights already. Maybe you are planning for Christmas.

# November

8

2011

## 1 TUESDAY
*Moon Age Day 5    Moon Sign Capricorn*

It's already the first day of November, and you may well be left wondering where much of the year has actually gone. However, if you look back you should see just how far you have come in many respects, and you can still plan events and happenings that will fall within this year. An optimistic approach works best today.

## 2 WEDNESDAY
*Moon Age Day 6    Moon Sign Aquarius*

All sorts of snippets of information are available today, and you need to keep watching and listening in order to make the most of them. Your personal objectives are very important at this stage and you needn't allow yourself to be sidelined in anything. Keep talking and make sure that everyone knows how you feel about things.

## 3 THURSDAY
*Moon Age Day 7    Moon Sign Aquarius*

There are signs that you may have your work cut out today in solving problems, particularly those that are caused by colleagues or even friends. You have what it takes to deal with most situations, and you can afford to approach life with a very positive attitude. If anyone is the joker in the pack around this time, it can certainly be you!

## 4 FRIDAY
*Moon Age Day 8    Moon Sign Aquarius*

It looks as though you have an opportunity to take a far more dominating approach to life now and with Mars in your solar fourth house this is likely to be especially true around home and family. Now is the time to show loved ones how you really feel about things, and that means not being in the least tardy when it comes to having your say.

## 5 SATURDAY
*Moon Age Day 9    Moon Sign Pisces*

Charisma on your part is emphasised, though there may be something of a dichotomy between the way you are behaving at home and out there in the social world. To family members you could seem quite bossy on occasions, whereas friends find you to be charming and easy to approach. Look towards your natural Taurean patience.

## 6 SUNDAY
*Moon Age Day 10    Moon Sign Pisces*

Intuition is strong, so that even if you are not getting on equally well with everyone in a verbal sense, you might know instinctively how they are likely to be thinking. The artistic side of your nature is to the fore at the moment, encouraging you to have very definite ideas about the way you want your surroundings to be, both now and for later.

## 7 MONDAY
*Moon Age Day 11    Moon Sign Aries*

Your personal life seems to be emphasised now, allowing you to concentrate on those issues that have potential to make you feel happier and more contented in the weeks and months ahead. Family discussions suit the present astrological scene, and there are positive gains to be made from knowing how others feel.

## 8 TUESDAY
*Moon Age Day 12    Moon Sign Aries*

Be prepared to deal with some powerful emotions, and to direct most of your thinking towards home and family. Beware of frayed tempers, and don't allow yourself to be accused of being bossy. Mars is in your solar fourth house, and that can indicate the possibility of a little temper being in evidence when you are at home.

## 9 WEDNESDAY
*Moon Age Day 13    Moon Sign Aries*

You might decide to slow things down somewhat whilst the Moon is in your solar twelfth house, but as always this comes ahead of a much more progressive period. From a positive point of view you will have time to work things out, and you needn't be pushed or harried for the moment. Be ready to respond if friends demand your attention.

# 10 THURSDAY
*Moon Age Day 14    Moon Sign Taurus*

The lunar high emphasises your impeccable sense of timing, assisting you to make headway in practical matters. It's time to move away from negative thoughts, and, on the contrary, to concentrate your mind on very positive issues to do with career and money. Capitalise on the stronger element of good luck that is available now.

# 11 FRIDAY
*Moon Age Day 15    Moon Sign Taurus*

Even if your mind is working overtime, you have sufficient energy at the moment for your body to keep up. Your health is favoured at present, and if there have been any issues in that direction recently, now would be an ideal time to resolve them. All things considered, this has potential to be the most positive time of the month for you.

# 12 SATURDAY
*Moon Age Day 16    Moon Sign Gemini*

Does today seem to be something of a let-down? If so, trends suggest that the essence of the way you feel is mental and emotional, rather than anything that is going wrong in a tangible sense. There are good reasons to keep pushing forward and to ignore the fact that you may be feeling slightly down.

# 13 SUNDAY
*Moon Age Day 17    Moon Sign Gemini*

Monetary improvements might now be within your grasp. These are a result of a combination of positive actions on your part and the way you make use of a little general good luck. Today could be profitable in other ways too, particularly if you can find the right sort of people to help you make up your mind about things.

# 14 MONDAY
*Moon Age Day 18    Moon Sign Gemini*

This can be a time of great insights, and your intuitive nature should be working overtime. When it comes to assessing others you will now be second to none, and you shouldn't be easily fooled, in either a practical or a personal sense. It's time to find out whether there is room for compromise regarding a disagreement in the family.

## 15 TUESDAY          *Moon Age Day 19    Moon Sign Cancer*

Today is about enjoying competition, and about your willingness to pit your wits against more or less anyone. Although Taurus is a fairly easy-going sort of zodiac sign, it is also the case that you like to win. At the moment this tendency is much emphasised, so don't be afraid to go to almost any length to be victorious.

## 16 WEDNESDAY        *Moon Age Day 20    Moon Sign Cancer*

Stimulation can now be obtained from those you meet socially, assisting you to formulate alternative strategies and ingenious ideas that were not in place only a day or two ago. Mentally speaking you should be as bright as a button and it would take someone extremely clever to fool you in any way. Your cognitive skills are to the fore.

## 17 THURSDAY         *Moon Age Day 21    Moon Sign Leo*

This may be a time of some restlessness, though not necessarily in a negative sense. If you really want to be active and enterprising, you probably won't be very happy with any circumstance that threatens to restrict you or hold you back. This could lead to a little testiness under some circumstances, though you need to ensure that your charm prevails.

## 18 FRIDAY           *Moon Age Day 22    Moon Sign Leo*

Mars has now moved on in your solar chart. This allows you to take some of the heat out of domestic relationships and to boost your own charisma. You might even be able to attract certain people who weren't too keen on you before, and to persuade even relative strangers to pay you significant attention.

## 19 SATURDAY         *Moon Age Day 23    Moon Sign Virgo*

This is a time of potential excitement and change – a period when you can't wait for others to keep up and when you should be ready to follow the dictates of your own will. Of course there are occasions when you can't ignore the needs of those around you. It's about using your present ingenuity to somehow incorporate them.

# 20 SUNDAY                    *Moon Age Day 24   Moon Sign Virgo*

For today at least the self-sacrificing side of your nature is emphasised, allowing you to focus on making those you love happy. You have what it takes to achieve greater peace on the home front than has been the case in recent weeks. Why not spend some time thinking about how important personal attachments are to you?

# 21 MONDAY                    *Moon Age Day 25   Moon Sign Virgo*

It's time to get yourself noticed, and to actively do things to make sure that you are not overlooked. When it comes to getting what you want in a professional sense, commitment and intent are both extremely important at the moment. It's a question of using your knowing knack of being in the right place at the most opportune time.

# 22 TUESDAY                   *Moon Age Day 26   Moon Sign Libra*

Be prepared to welcome people you don't see very often back into your life again now. They may be able to provide some interesting new speculations regarding matters that you thought were dead and buried. If you find the attitude of some friends slightly puzzling, this would be an ideal time to try to get to the bottom of a number of issues.

# 23 WEDNESDAY                 *Moon Age Day 27   Moon Sign Libra*

Life is not a rehearsal, as you may be about to discover. Instead of waiting around to see what might happen, today is a time to get busy and to make things mature in the way you would wish. There is no end to your own power under present trends, but it all depends on your own attitude and your willingness to become involved.

# 24 THURSDAY   ☿   *Moon Age Day 28   Moon Sign Scorpio*

This may not be the luckiest day of the month, especially in any practical sense. You have the lunar low to cope with, and this might encourage you to slow things down in a number of different ways. It's worth relying on what others can do for you and taking some rest. You can get back up to speed soon, but rushing today won't help.

## 25 FRIDAY ☿ *Moon Age Day 0   Moon Sign Scorpio*

This is another day that more or less demands you take things at a calmer pace and don't get involved in issues that are going to take all your energy to resolve. Energy may well be in short supply at the moment, which is why you need to watch and wait. By tomorrow you can get things back to normal but for the moment you can afford to relax.

## 26 SATURDAY ☿ *Moon Age Day 1   Moon Sign Sagittarius*

If you really want something from life today you need to get involved. The lunar low is well out of the way and your usual strength and resilience should be much more in focus. Issues that are finished and done with need to be ignored, whilst you commit yourself to new situations. Lady Luck may offer you some extra incentives at this time.

## 27 SUNDAY ☿ *Moon Age Day 2   Moon Sign Sagittarius*

Don't be distracted by the demands made upon you by friends and family members. Although you may have time to think about domestic issues on a Sunday, at the same time there is plenty of potential excitement about too. Your best response is to split your day, but avoid giving yourself entirely to anything tedious or demanding.

## 28 MONDAY ☿ *Moon Age Day 3   Moon Sign Capricorn*

Now is a good time to take stock of where you are actually going – as well as wondering whether some of these directions are either necessary or desirable. You should certainly be standing up for your rights around now, as well as backing up those who don't have a very loud voice when it comes to defending their own interests.

## 29 TUESDAY ☿ *Moon Age Day 4   Moon Sign Capricorn*

Right at this moment in time the focus is on your wish to be number one. Since you rarely have a selfish bone in your body there is nothing at all wrong with being self-centred once in a while. What's more, you should be able to convince those who care about you the most to let you have your own way. Even some strangers might join in!

# 30 WEDNESDAY ☿ *Moon Age Day 5 Moon Sign Aquarius*

Trends highlight your intellectual hunger, and you can use this to find out what lies around every bend in the road ahead of you. You may also decide to travel more and to seek out fascinating destinations that haven't occurred to you previously. It might not be the best time of year to be setting off somewhere – but who cares?

# (8) *December* 2011

## 1 THURSDAY    ☿   *Moon Age Day 6   Moon Sign Aquarius*

You should now be able to take advantage of a winning streak in a professional sense and this is a favourable time to act upon new opportunities that you have identified. The first day of December could turn out to be quite exciting and to offer possibilities that would have seemed out of the question, even a few short months ago.

## 2 FRIDAY    ☿   *Moon Age Day 7   Moon Sign Pisces*

You can be a good listener today, which isn't at all unusual for Taurus but is especially enhanced whilst the Moon occupies its present position in the zodiac. It's time to persuade friends to spill the beans regarding issues you may not have understood at all well before, and there are undoubtedly some surprises in store.

## 3 SATURDAY    ☿   *Moon Age Day 8   Moon Sign Pisces*

Seeking adventure continues to be the name of the game, though now you can do so through romance. If you have more than one admirer at the moment, this could call for some sort of balancing act. Even Taurus subjects who feel themselves to be settled in a romantic sense could get the flame of love to burn much brighter.

## 4 SUNDAY    ☿   *Moon Age Day 9   Moon Sign Pisces*

Don't be afraid to leave behind anything that is dragging you down. This might seem the worst time of the year for the usual type of spring-clean, but as far as your mind goes, this is the best period of all. A new year is not very far away and you don't want to carry too much surplus baggage on towards the end of December.

## 5 MONDAY ☿ *Moon Age Day 10 Moon Sign Aries*

The Sun is now in your solar eighth house and that assists you to achieve a certain amount of change in your life. These are not situations that are beyond your control but rather ones you are choosing for yourself. New plans and life-goals are within your grasp, and there is plenty of room for your own opinions, which count now more than ever.

## 6 TUESDAY ☿ *Moon Age Day 11 Moon Sign Aries*

You have what it takes to move forward, particularly at work, even if other people seem to be dragging their feet. It seems as if there is no stopping you just now, and you can rise to challenges in a moment. This is an ideal time to make changes at home, so why not make some alterations in preparation for Christmas?

## 7 WEDNESDAY ☿ *Moon Age Day 12 Moon Sign Taurus*

You can now afford to be competitive and to take on challenges that you might have avoided earlier in the year. The lunar high offers you greater incentive and assists you to make full use of the energy you have available. New and inventive strategies can be put into place, both in a practical sense and in terms of relationships.

## 8 THURSDAY ☿ *Moon Age Day 13 Moon Sign Taurus*

Not only is your optimism emphasised at the moment, you also have scope to be very giving in your attitude. There should be time enough to get what you want from life but also to give someone else a leg up too. A perfect time to meet new people, some of whom might prove to be of great use to you in the days and weeks to come.

## 9 FRIDAY ☿ *Moon Age Day 14 Moon Sign Taurus*

It looks as though new opportunities and fresh horizons continue to be of supreme importance to you as this working week draws to a close. With the weekend in view you might decide to plan something quite startling in a social sense. Personal attachments can definitely be strengthened under present planetary trends.

## 10 SATURDAY  ☿  *Moon Age Day 15   Moon Sign Gemini*

Your love of travel is emphasised now, so you may well feel dull and disinterested if you don't manage to create some change in almost every aspect of your life. What started out as a little restlessness has now become something much bigger. It's time to avoid unnecessary routines and opt for as many diversions as you can find.

## 11 SUNDAY  ☿  *Moon Age Day 16   Moon Sign Gemini*

A little soul searching may be necessary in order for you to come to terms with certain aspects of your life as they appear now. In your anxiety to make almost everything different, there is a very real chance you might throw out the baby with the bathwater. You might have to put on the brakes a little after making conscious decisions.

## 12 MONDAY  ☿  *Moon Age Day 17   Moon Sign Cancer*

You can best avoid conflicts in your love life by refusing to get involved in pointless discussions or even arguments. Even if it isn't you who is being reactive but rather those around you, it's easy to get drawn into rows. For most of the time you are as calm and easy-going as anything, but you do sometimes display a stubborn streak.

## 13 TUESDAY  ☿  *Moon Age Day 18   Moon Sign Cancer*

An entire change of scenery would be a fantastic option for Taurus today. The Sun is still there in your solar eighth house, giving you every encouragement to seek out something new. Your best response to this situation is to be as flexible as possible. The trouble starts if you insist on keeping everything the way it has always been.

## 14 WEDNESDAY ☿  *Moon Age Day 19   Moon Sign Leo*

Today could be especially favourable for business matters, since you display a healthy mix of optimism and caution. This is Taurus at its best and it stands you in good stead when it comes to strengthening finances. Planning projects should be easy, and you can use the understanding you presently have with colleagues to convince them to follow your lead.

## 15 THURSDAY
*Moon Age Day 20    Moon Sign Leo*

A sense of co-operation that probably didn't exist a few days ago now makes itself felt. Maintaining an upbeat emotional outlook should help you to avoid getting involved in disputes that lead to arguments. The Moon is in your solar fourth house at the moment, giving you the assistance you need in dealings with your family.

## 16 FRIDAY
*Moon Age Day 21    Moon Sign Leo*

Romance could bring a little tension on this particular Friday, and you will need to be careful not to take offence over something that isn't really very important. If you are faced with challenges at work, you need to look for the positive aspects. It's important for the moment not to react too harshly to nothing in particular.

## 17 SATURDAY
*Moon Age Day 22    Moon Sign Virgo*

A personal issue may show the extent to which you have your work cut out. This could be quite a reactive sort of weekend, but you can still make progress and enjoy yourself if you approach matters in the right way. Stop and think before you make momentous decisions, and do your best to avoid cluttering up your life with pointless things.

## 18 SUNDAY
*Moon Age Day 23    Moon Sign Virgo*

Professional progress is now possible, that is if you happen to work at the weekend, but otherwise this can be a fairly steady sort of day. There is much to be said for preparing yourself for the upcoming festivities and for enjoying a fairly settled family time if you can. Restlessness is still symptomatic of this period.

## 19 MONDAY
*Moon Age Day 24    Moon Sign Libra*

Your strength lies in your inner drive to make a good impression all round. Meeting new people counts for a great deal now, and it's worth putting in some extra effort to make the most of what could turn out to be deep friendships. Beware of getting too involved in the personal problems of friends. By all means give advice, but stay away from intrigue!

## 20 TUESDAY
*Moon Age Day 25    Moon Sign Libra*

Today is important, not really for its own sake but because the lunar low arrives tomorrow. Be prepared to put a full stop to any jobs that have been going on for a while and that now need to be finished. It's time to clear the decks for action you are planning for the Christmas period, and to ensure you pay attention to detail when at work.

## 21 WEDNESDAY
*Moon Age Day 26    Moon Sign Scorpio*

Life can sometimes be disappointing, and today could be a time of missed opportunities, or at least that's how it might seem as the lunar low arrives. The truth is that if you are not your usual optimistic self you will tend to look on the black side of things. Just watch and wait because your moment will come, and maybe sooner than you think.

## 22 THURSDAY
*Moon Age Day 27    Moon Sign Scorpio*

If it seems as though you have more than your average number of worries, you need to ask yourself whether this is really the case. Most problems that come with the lunar low tend to turn out as phantoms – and they disappear as quickly as they arrived. Fortunately, your sense of humour is still intact, so when you laugh today make sure it is at yourself.

## 23 FRIDAY
*Moon Age Day 28    Moon Sign Sagittarius*

You have scope to tap into some strong support today, particularly when you are at work. This has potential to be a busy time, though that isn't too surprising with Christmas only a couple of days away. Take some time out to remember all those people for whom you haven't yet bought presents and do something about it today.

## 24 SATURDAY
*Moon Age Day 29    Moon Sign Sagittarius*

Trends indicate that social issues might now have less attraction for you, particularly if you have a lot to do behind the scenes. If you are going out tonight, make sure everything is in place at home before you go. It would be very easy to get carried away, forget the time and end up getting home later than you planned!

## 25 SUNDAY          *Moon Age Day 0    Moon Sign Capricorn*

There are strong indications for travel in your chart at this time. This could suggest that many Taureans are choosing to spend Christmas away from home, or else visiting relatives and friends during the day. Family trends are perhaps not very favourable, and even if you are fine yourself, you may well have to deal with disagreements close by.

## 26 MONDAY          *Moon Age Day 1    Moon Sign Capricorn*

Romantic issues may throw up the odd challenge and you need to be paying attention in order to make certain you are saying and doing the right things. It might seem as if there are 'tests' around now, custom-made to ensure that you are thinking and acting in the right way. New hobbies or pastimes are well accented now.

## 27 TUESDAY          *Moon Age Day 2    Moon Sign Aquarius*

Intimate relationships could prove to be rather demanding once again. What this actually means will differ from person to person, but it is influenced by the position of Mercury, which now occupies your solar eighth house. This supports restlessness and a desire for change, but it also gives 'finality' to some of the things you say.

## 28 WEDNESDAY          *Moon Age Day 3    Moon Sign Aquarius*

Your interest in travel, which has been increasingly highlighted throughout this month, could now become intense. This would be an ideal time to seek fresh fields and pastures new, even if those around you have very different ideas. Take short trips by all means, though what you really want is a long and luxurious holiday. Some chance!

## 29 THURSDAY          *Moon Age Day 4    Moon Sign Pisces*

Perhaps fortunately, the spotlight is now on your social life. If there has been a lull since Christmas Day, bear in mind that this might have been inspired more by your state of mind than by any external situation. Be prepared to spend time with your friends and to make the most of opportunities to do something completely new and different.

## 30 FRIDAY
*Moon Age Day 5    Moon Sign Pisces*

Mars is now in your solar fifth house, offering high spirits in the romantic sphere, and indicating an end to the year that can be positively explosive when it comes to love. You have what it takes to improve your popularity and to give a good impression of yourself, no matter where you happen to be. However, a lack of patience is possible.

## 31 SATURDAY
*Moon Age Day 6    Moon Sign Pisces*

In terms of actual progress, today could get off to a fairly slow start. Don't worry if this is the case because you can speed things up gradually as the hours pass. Why not let others do some of the planning for tonight, while you make yourself look beautiful and get yourself prepared to stun everyone? Just be willing to let go and to have a good time.

# TAURUS:
# 2012 DIARY PAGES

# TAURUS:
# YOUR YEAR IN BRIEF

The start of the year, during January and February, is likely to be a cautious time for you. This is often the case for the zodiac sign of Taurus and under the prevailing circumstances this year is no exception. The fact that you are exercising a little self-discipline and organising yourself rather more than usual means that your ultimate success rate is likely to be that much greater.

March and April find you committing yourself to new ventures, anxious to make a good impression on all sorts of people, but at the same time showing that wonderful, warm nature that lies at the heart of your personality. Although there are some periods of slight stress, in the main you take life in your stride and show an inspirational and even a dynamic face to the world at large.

May and June are likely to be quiet for you, though the less progressive periods are interspersed with times of high activity and a desire for progress. Finances should strengthen at this time and you will find yourself more than willing to try out fresh ideas. Some Taurus people might be thinking about new job opportunities at this point in the year and can gain from listening to some good advice, particularly from special friends.

July and August are eventful months and ones that see you regularly on the move. All romantic associations are positive and strong around now, offering you new incentives and the chance to broaden your horizons professionally, personally and also romantically. It is at this time that some slightly pushy, and sometimes even bossy, qualities begin to show more than would normally be the case for Taurus. You should take every opportunity this month to make changes in and around your home.

It is possible that the autumn will find you in a less positive frame of mind and there are specifically times in late September and early October when it might not seem that there are many interesting events happening in your life. Keep trying because these trends pass soon enough. Good personal relationships bolster your spirits at this time and new friends should be entering your life.

It looks as though the final part of the year will be a mixed bag, with the emphasis on continued success in personal and practical endeavours and an ability to get what you want from life. Try to be as flexible as you can, and to give other people the benefit of the doubt. Christmas may be more traditional than usual, but enjoyable all the same. You should commence the New Year with a great sense of optimism and feeling that 2012 has been both useful and enjoyable in great measure.

# January 2012

## 1 SUNDAY
*Moon Age Day 7    Moon Sign Aries*

You start the New Year with the Moon in your solar twelfth house and this is going to slightly undermine your will to achieve, so probably not the most dynamic day you will encounter during 2012. On the other hand you should be in a very peaceful and quite contemplative frame of mind so today is definitely good for thinking.

## 2 MONDAY
*Moon Age Day 8    Moon Sign Aries*

Inspiration, meaning and personal success are all there for the taking, even if the going seems a little difficult at first today. It's quite likely you will be away from work right now and in all probability you will be planning your next moves, rather than putting them into action. Loved ones should be quite attentive now.

## 3 TUESDAY
*Moon Age Day 9    Moon Sign Taurus*

The Moon has now moved into your own zodiac sign of Taurus and brings with it the period of the month known as the lunar high. This means you will be on top form and anxious to take any bull by the horns. There could hardly be a better set of circumstances for what amounts to the first working day of a new year.

## 4 WEDNESDAY
*Moon Age Day 10    Moon Sign Taurus*

Your intuitive abilities are stimulated today so use them to outwit any competition that is around you. You head towards your chosen targets quickly and show a very positive face to the practical world. Meanwhile, you are also working on forging stronger relationships and creating a better general understanding at home.

# 5 THURSDAY
*Moon Age Day 11    Moon Sign Taurus*

Highly intellectual activity is favoured today and you can tackle situations that might have seemed confusing or somehow beyond you just a few weeks ago. Although it will take time during January to get exactly what you want, Taureans are generally fairly patient, so you are happy to move forward steadily towards your objectives.

# 6 FRIDAY
*Moon Age Day 12    Moon Sign Gemini*

You could be feeling more creative and expressive than you have lately. If so, you need to cater for these trends by taking on something new and by finding new ways to communicate to the world at large. People you haven't seen for quite some time are now likely to appear in your life again – like a bolt from the blue.

# 7 SATURDAY
*Moon Age Day 13    Moon Sign Gemini*

Conversations you have with others are likely to have a profound effect on the way you are thinking and could cause you to make an occasional u-turn. Don't worry if you have to change a few plans because what you are doing is repositioning yourself in the light of changing circumstances. Get onside with friends with big ideas.

# 8 SUNDAY
*Moon Age Day 14    Moon Sign Cancer*

You can now more easily advance both your professional and domestic goals with the help of authority figures or new business contacts. On a personal note, you should be getting on especially well with people who have recently come into your life, as well as working towards deepening your sense of security in existing attachments.

# 9 MONDAY
*Moon Age Day 15    Moon Sign Cancer*

The Sun is in your solar ninth house and it is true that this can sometimes bring a degree of dissatisfaction with how things are in your life, so you may be thinking about trying to change things for the better. However, not all your plans may work out quite the way you would wish and your usual steady approach is likely to work best.

## 10 TUESDAY          *Moon Age Day 16   Moon Sign Cancer*

Make sure you enjoy all the benefits of your domestic set-up, while at the same time injecting a little excitement if you wish. If any members of your family have ideas on home improvements, listen carefully to what they have to say. Co-operative ventures work well now, particularly in a domestic setting.

## 11 WEDNESDAY          *Moon Age Day 17   Moon Sign Leo*

Taurus people like to plan ahead, and you could find this a particularly auspicious day to exercise your far-sightedness. You are likely to have a good idea what you want from life and how to get it. This might not be the best day for actually starting a new project at work unless you have significant support from colleagues.

## 12 THURSDAY          *Moon Age Day 18   Moon Sign Leo*

A sense of personal triumph and a big boost to your ego can be expected around now. It seems as though you are doing everything right, but remember that pride can go before a fall so don't be to arrogant in your opinions. You have a great sense of what looks right at the moment so use it to present yourself in the best possible way.

## 13 FRIDAY          *Moon Age Day 19   Moon Sign Virgo*

That instinctive ability to use co-operation to your own advantage isn't quite as strong today and tomorrow as it was a few days ago. You might misunderstand exactly what others want or try to influence them too much. It would be sensible to keep yourself to yourself if you know there is potential for disagreements or arguments.

## 14 SATURDAY          *Moon Age Day 20   Moon Sign Virgo*

If you are looking for backing from others you may have to ask for it. Don't expect things to fall into your lap at the moment; you may need to put in some extra effort, especially socially. Your romantic prospects are positive, however, so make sure you are well positioned to take advantage of them. This is not a Saturday night to stay in.

# 15 SUNDAY
*Moon Age Day 21    Moon Sign Libra*

Personal fulfilment isn't too easy to find under present trends and there could be a kind of restlessness around you that is difficult to control. Take the initiative and deal with it by getting out of the house and doing something different. This is certainly not the best day for sitting around and waiting for things to happen.

# 16 MONDAY
*Moon Age Day 22    Moon Sign Libra*

A break from everyday routine is called for as you are likely to be feeling restless again and inclined to look for fresh fields and pastures new. That's fine for today but won't be so likely tomorrow. If there are new incentives to deal with at work, so much the better, but prepare yourself for a couple of much quieter days ahead.

# 17 TUESDAY
*Moon Age Day 23    Moon Sign Scorpio*

You are likely to find this a fairly challenging time. This is because the Moon is now in your opposite zodiac sign of Scorpio. This period, which lasts for about two days each month, is called the lunar low and it tends to sap your energy. At the same time you may find it more difficult than usual to get other people to co-operate with what you want.

# 18 WEDNESDAY
*Moon Age Day 24    Moon Sign Scorpio*

Beware of building up unrealistic expectations and make sure that you have plans firmly nailed down before you go ahead with any new projects. In reality today is best for planning, leaving the major actions until another day. If you take time to observe rather than rushing forward, today could actually be quite rewarding.

# 19 THURSDAY
*Moon Age Day 25    Moon Sign Sagittarius*

You should feel quite relaxed and unfettered today, so capitalise on the influences, especially socially. It may become possible to do something you have wanted to do for some time, and you may not have to put in anywhere near the effort you expected. It's a good time to look ahead to the summer and make plans for distant travel.

## 20 FRIDAY      *Moon Age Day 26   Moon Sign Sagittarius*

It is just possible that today you will put your own desires ahead of those of other people in your immediate circle. It isn't like Taurus to be selfish but you should have the courage of your convictions if you are sure that what you want will also benefit those around you. This is likely to be the case for the next few weeks.

## 21 SATURDAY      *Moon Age Day 27   Moon Sign Capricorn*

You could now begin to feel a strong competitive streak that makes you stand your ground, perhaps in practical situations or especially in sporting activities. This makes you a formidable opponent and your natural Taurean stubbornness will be showing. You simply won't budge unless it's in your own interests.

## 22 SUNDAY      *Moon Age Day 28   Moon Sign Capricorn*

Venus is now in your solar eleventh house, which means you'll generally be feeling good about yourself. It makes social encounters that much more enjoyable and means love and romance should be going well for you. All kinds of group activities are likely to work well today and through the coming week.

## 23 MONDAY      *Moon Age Day 0   Moon Sign Capricorn*

You should be feeling very positive at the start of this working week and have a sound and intuitive sense of how best to communicate with your colleagues. Those Taurus subjects who are in full-time education should be getting on especially well, even if circumstances force some sort of changes that make you feel uneasy.

## 24 TUESDAY      *Moon Age Day 1   Moon Sign Aquarius*

There could be new friendships for you, possibly associated with work. There are definite benefits to be gained right now from mixing business with pleasure and someone you either didn't know well before or who you did not care for is now likely to take a more prominent role in your life, both at work and socially.

## 25 WEDNESDAY     *Moon Age Day 2   Moon Sign Aquarius*

You are likely to enjoy a great deal of emotional energy now so you'll find it easy to tell your lover exactly how you feel about them. Make sure you channel your efforts in sensible directions and leave vague schemes to other people. Your instincts are strong so trust them to help you decide which course of action is the one to follow.

## 26 THURSDAY     *Moon Age Day 3   Moon Sign Pisces*

Handling major responsibilities is not difficult for you under present trends. Others recognise this fact, which is why you are being singled out for special treatment by colleagues or superiors. If you are between jobs at the moment, you'll find the trends should help to make you feel more optimistic about your job hunting.

## 27 FRIDAY     *Moon Age Day 4   Moon Sign Pisces*

At the moment you are likely to make friends easily, so you can add significantly to your social life now by joining some new groups or organisations. You could be confronted by more choices than is comfortable for your conservative nature. Just stop and think before you make any major commitments.

## 28 SATURDAY     *Moon Age Day 5   Moon Sign Aries*

Gradual expansion towards future growth starts to look more possible than it was at the beginning of January but don't be too hasty. The best way forward is to stay calm and relaxed and not to take anything for granted. Patience is the very virtue that makes Taurus such a formidable zodiac sign.

## 29 SUNDAY     *Moon Age Day 6   Moon Sign Aries*

An emotional matter is likely to demand your attention on this particular Sunday but if you don't feel qualified to make a judgement, watch and wait. This is not a good time to become involved in arguments and it would be far better to let others disagree than to get yourself into situations that won't help you at all.

## 30 MONDAY

*Moon Age Day 7    Moon Sign Aries*

A quieter day ahead of the lunar high allows you to sit back and take stock as the Moon passes through your solar twelfth house. You should be feeling quite mellow and you won't want to upset anyone right now. On the contrary, you will be doing everything you can to keep people as happy as proves to be possible.

## 31 TUESDAY

*Moon Age Day 8    Moon Sign Taurus*

Newer and better opportunities come your way now, thanks to the arrival of the lunar high. With a greater level of physical energy and a determination that is going off the scale, this is the time to get what you want from life. Routines are definitely not for you on this particular day and you will want to make some sweeping changes.

## 1 WEDNESDAY
*Moon Age Day 9   Moon Sign Taurus*

Now you need to be thinking big and making the most of what nature and the planets are offering you. Don't stop any projects half way through but keep going until you get exactly what you want. Your popularity should be high so now is also the best time to ask people for favours. They are unlikely to refuse you.

## 2 THURSDAY
*Moon Age Day 10   Moon Sign Gemini*

When it comes to career developments you should be at your best right now but you will need to rely on the good offices of those around you. This should not be difficult because you are generally very popular and people actively want to lend a hand. Beware of getting involved in very complicated situations at home.

## 3 FRIDAY
*Moon Age Day 11   Moon Sign Gemini*

This could turn out to be an all-or-nothing time, so before you get cracking with any new incentives or plans, make sure that you can see them through. You should have plenty of energy but be realistic about what you can achieve or you could bite off more than you can chew and end up exhausted. Watch out for the start of new interests.

## 4 SATURDAY
*Moon Age Day 12   Moon Sign Gemini*

There are plenty of benefits to be derived from social situations now, and the influences are good for your love life too. That means this is definitely not a stay-at-home weekend. Get out of the house and have some fun. Life's practicalities can wait for another time.

## 5 SUNDAY
*Moon Age Day 13   Moon Sign Cancer*

You always have a great deal of self-control and self-discipline, so you tend not to gamble or take too many risks. That may be safe but it also means you can miss opportunities. This is especially true at the moment and you are certainly not likely to gamble. But watch out for new and better opportunities that may shake your resolve.

## 6 MONDAY
*Moon Age Day 14   Moon Sign Cancer*

Due to increased enthusiasm, energetic initiative and the ability to cope under professional pressure, you should get on extremely well today. You can make an especially good impression on people in charge and there isn't much doubt about the fact that people are watching you with great respect around this time.

## 7 TUESDAY
*Moon Age Day 15   Moon Sign Leo*

Much that is truly rewarding and meaningful centres around the home. Meanwhile, issues from the past tend to predominate and this would be a very good time for seeking out old faces and places. You should also be in contact with people who live at a considerable distance or with whom you have lost touch recently.

## 8 WEDNESDAY
*Moon Age Day 16   Moon Sign Leo*

You remain very keen to be accommodating and to help out those around you as much as possible, although there may be some issues of little real importance that bring out your stubborn side. Try to be as flexible as possible. Maintain your sense of perspective so you can laugh off unimportant obstacles.

## 9 THURSDAY
*Moon Age Day 17   Moon Sign Virgo*

There is a developing need for you to be the centre of attention, which is not really typical for Taurus, so it should certainly cause people to sit up and take notice of your abilities. Uncharacteristically, you may even be performing in some sort of public arena. Do take advantage of the favourable influences to show what you can do.

## 10 FRIDAY
*Moon Age Day 18    Moon Sign Virgo*

Focus on what needs bringing to the surface as far as your love life is concerned and don't get too preoccupied with matters that are of no real consequence. You do need to show how much you understand your partner and to be willing to listen to something they have to say, even if it seems irrelevant to you.

## 11 SATURDAY
*Moon Age Day 19    Moon Sign Libra*

If you make the right moves today it could substantially benefit your future potential. If you work at the weekend, then so much the better. Socially, you may be slightly restricted by the actions and opinions of people around you. In the end, it will be up to you to make the running and to let other people catch up later.

## 12 SUNDAY
*Moon Age Day 20    Moon Sign Libra*

Whatever you want to achieve this month is likely to feature heavily on your mind around this time. You are putting in that extra bit of effort that can make all the difference and showing a very positive face to the world in a general sense. Make the most of it as things may not seem quite so straightforward once the new week starts.

## 13 MONDAY
*Moon Age Day 21    Moon Sign Scorpio*

The lunar low could slow things down significantly at the start of this working week and is going to make it more difficult for you to make the grade in some respects. You will have a much more satisfying start to the week if you recognise your present limitations and work within them rather than aiming too high.

## 14 TUESDAY
*Moon Age Day 22    Moon Sign Scorpio*

Be careful not to push yourself more than is necessary and stick to what you know instead of going off at a tangent. It may be true that others might seem to be getting ahead while you don't have the answers you need. Be patient. You don't always have to achieve – people like your company and you are a nice person to be around.

## 15 WEDNESDAY     *Moon Age Day 23    Moon Sign Scorpio*

If it appears that life is determined to throw obstacles in your path, you can be reasonably sure that this apparent tendency will be gone by the middle of the day. After that, you respond to more positive planetary influences and should be able to get moving on projects that seem to have been stalled for some time.

## 16 THURSDAY     *Moon Age Day 24    Moon Sign Sagittarius*

What is really important at the moment is to try to see other people's points of view. Fortunately, this is something you are instinctively good at, so you can put your strong empathy to good use. It may take you some time to explain something to a person who has difficulty with new things but your patience will be rewarded.

## 17 FRIDAY     *Moon Age Day 25    Moon Sign Sagittarius*

If you are presented with several different ways forward today it is important to keep your options open and not to respond to the first possibility. In some situations you might decide to conserve your energy and make a conscious decision not to show your full resources for the moment. This could turn out to be very wise.

## 18 SATURDAY     *Moon Age Day 26    Moon Sign Capricorn*

A potentially important phase is now at hand, with the emphasis on a strong learning curve. Since the relevant planets are moving very slowly at this time, you can go on taking in new information for quite some time. Fortunately for you, Taurus is the sort of zodiac sign that has almost endless patience, so use it well.

## 19 SUNDAY     *Moon Age Day 27    Moon Sign Capricorn*

This is a harmonious time for social relationships so take this opportunity to resolve any differences of opinion there may have been between yourself and other family members. Today's trends are great for teamwork, too, and for building a new platform from which you can operate more efficiently in the future.

## 20 MONDAY         *Moon Age Day 28    Moon Sign Aquarius*

The strong focus on work continues and there isn't much doubt that you have the potential to impress people, as well as finding new ways to tackle existing problems. This may mean pushing people out of their comfort zone, which might not be met with universal approval, but if you persevere the results will speak for themselves.

## 21 TUESDAY         *Moon Age Day 29    Moon Sign Aquarius*

Some relationships could feel as though they are more trouble than they are worth, especially if you constantly have to put yourself out for a so-called friend who seems to do nothing but insult you. But watch out for new social possibilities on the way. It may be that you have simply outgrown one or two relationships from the past.

## 22 WEDNESDAY         *Moon Age Day 0    Moon Sign Pisces*

Today is a good day to meet up with friends and acquaintances and, if you get out and socialise, it will break up some of that dull mid-week routine. Think carefully about what you want to do with your spare time and use it to have fun. Family commitments will still be there when you return but you need a break.

## 23 THURSDAY         *Moon Age Day 1    Moon Sign Pisces*

The strong social influences continue so keep your diary full. You may also discover that your love life is improving – even if you seem to have done little to promote the change. Keep up your efforts to streamline something at work but try not to make yourself unpopular by giving the impression you are working too hard.

## 24 FRIDAY         *Moon Age Day 2    Moon Sign Pisces*

Not a bad day to adopt a slightly lower profile today but not because the planets are working against your best interests. There are interludes when Earth signs such as yours need to reflect and to meditate and this could be one of them. By the evening you should be up to speed again so try to spend time enjoying yourself with friends.

## 25 SATURDAY
*Moon Age Day 3    Moon Sign Aries*

Although this is likely to be a generally happy period, the weekend could prove quieter than you might have expected. This is because the Moon is passing through your solar twelfth house, which is almost certain to make you more reflective. You'll still be bright and cheerful but may want to use the influences to do some thinking.

## 26 SUNDAY
*Moon Age Day 4    Moon Sign Aries*

If life throws you into the path of someone you really admire, make the most of the situation rather than shying away and feeling that you have no right to be involved with them. At a personal level you are much more talented than you believe so grab the chance to prove it at some stage during Sunday if the opportunity arises.

## 27 MONDAY
*Moon Age Day 5    Moon Sign Taurus*

You could be feeling highly intuitive today and know instinctively how others are going to behave. This – and the fact that this is a lucky time for you – should help you make the most of any opportunities that arise. In love, there's everything to play for so put yourself in the right places to find an exciting new romance.

## 28 TUESDAY
*Moon Age Day 6    Moon Sign Taurus*

You are as energetic as you could possibly be, so direct that energy to fulfil your prime objectives. Events seem to fall into place perfectly without much effort, and this is the very opposite of one of those days when you can't seem to do anything right. Test your luck and don't be afraid to put yourself forward because now you are a winner.

## 29 WEDNESDAY
*Moon Age Day 7    Moon Sign Taurus*

Don't forget that there is an extra day this month and it's one you can definitely use to your advantage. Arrange to spend Leap Year Day in good company and amongst individuals who are useful to you in terms of your own plans. When you are feeling good, you look good, and you should have no difficulty turning heads.

(8)

# March

2012

## 1 THURSDAY
*Moon Age Day 8   Moon Sign Gemini*

If you feel highly charged emotionally today, then turn your attention to improving your relationships, old or new. Before the day is very old you should have the chance to form a new attachment that may seem superficial but could prove to be more important later. Money matters should seem quite settled now.

## 2 FRIDAY
*Moon Age Day 9   Moon Sign Gemini*

This is definitely a time for enjoying the company of other people and for making the most of what attachments can offer you in a practical sense. Not everyone is going to find you flavour of the month but you can't expect to be loved by the whole world. When it matters, most people will come good for you and show support.

## 3 SATURDAY
*Moon Age Day 10   Moon Sign Cancer*

There is the possibility of misunderstanding in some of what you say and do at the moment, which is why it is so important to explain yourself carefully and fully. There are strong social trends about and you may decide that a journey of some sort would be good. Even if you only get into town to do some shopping, you'll enjoy yourself.

## 4 SUNDAY
*Moon Age Day 11   Moon Sign Cancer*

The influences suggest an active and enterprising few months ahead, so it's a good time to begin to determine what sort of changes you want to make in your life. Plan for the summer especially and don't forget to make travel a part of what you have in mind. Keep in touch with friends who live a long way from you.

# 5 MONDAY
*Moon Age Day 12    Moon Sign Leo*

The planetary influences are shining on all group activities and you should not find it hard right now to be one of a team. You may not be the leader but you will be essential all the same. This would be an especially good time to join something and to get involved in new hobbies or pastimes.

# 6 TUESDAY
*Moon Age Day 13    Moon Sign Leo*

This is a great time for you, with plenty of positive energies around, making you look and feel good about yourself. Don't waste it; show the world how good you are. If romance is on your agenda, which it may well be under this planetary influence, then your timing is great because you have what it takes to turn heads wherever you go.

# 7 WEDNESDAY
*Moon Age Day 14    Moon Sign Leo*

Communication needs to be direct and explicit right now. You won't get anywhere by being coy or by beating about the bush. What is more, if you give your opinions clearly in group situations, that will be the best way to avoid confusion. People really do want to know what is on your mind and they respect your views.

# 8 THURSDAY
*Moon Age Day 15    Moon Sign Virgo*

Feeling generally at ease with yourself, this ought to be a good day and one that offers new incentives of a sort you perhaps were not expecting. The energies are still good for romance, and Taureans who have been looking for love could so easily find it around now. Venus stays where it is for a while and that means the future is bright.

# 9 FRIDAY
*Moon Age Day 16    Moon Sign Virgo*

You will gain the most by keeping your focus on love and pleasure. Taurus always wants to look right and this is a good time for giving a great deal of thought to your appearance both in and out of work. You might find routine particularly annoying now, in which case find ways to break out of the rut and make some changes.

## 10 SATURDAY    *Moon Age Day 17    Moon Sign Libra*

Use the extra energy you should be experiencing at the moment to tackle situations that might have caused you some trouble in the past. Don't get too tied up with details today but instead be willing to remain flexible in everything you do. It's a good day to show those close to you just how warm and romantic you can be.

## 11 SUNDAY    *Moon Age Day 18    Moon Sign Libra*

You should still be on good form and need to make the best of today because by tomorrow you are up against the lunar low. Anything dynamic that needs doing quickly should be undertaken now, in the knowledge that life will slow down somewhat over the next few days. Look to your social life today.

## 12 MONDAY    ☿    *Moon Age Day 19    Moon Sign Scorpio*

There could be a shift in the accent at work, with people behaving in a less than typical way and with you not displaying the drive and energy that have been so much a part of your nature recently. Be prepared to let others take the strain, while you sit back and watch for a while. You may not feel very positive in your attitude.

## 13 TUESDAY    ☿    *Moon Age Day 20    Moon Sign Scorpio*

Use this time to look at your life more carefully and discard any entanglements that are no longer necessary. By tomorrow you will be back in gear and raring to go but today would be better spent in reflection. The lunar low is unlikely to have a negative bearing on your love life, which should continue to shine.

## 14 WEDNESDAY ☿ *Moon Age Day 21    Moon Sign Sagittarius*

Venus is still shining her special light on you, bestowing you with a greater sense of social interaction and making it less difficult for you to get your message across. You might even be called extrovert by those around you; not something that is generally said of Taurus, which usually has a natural reserve.

88

## 15 THURSDAY  ☿ *Moon Age Day 22   Moon Sign Sagittarius*

What you need most of all today is to do something that specifically pleases you so don't be afraid to be slightly selfish. Of course you won't want to let others down but you won't have to. You can still achieve a sense of proportion, even though you are putting yourself forward a little more than usual. Stand by for some positive feedback.

## 16 FRIDAY  ☿ *Moon Age Day 23   Moon Sign Capricorn*

It is possible that a few of your ideas are drying up and need to be replaced with new ones. That means getting your thinking cap on, something that isn't at all difficult today. When work is out of the way, find new ways to have fun. This isn't the best time of year to be out of doors but it might figure somehow in your plans in any case.

## 17 SATURDAY  ☿ *Moon Age Day 24   Moon Sign Capricorn*

This may be an unusual Saturday. Though there seem to be plenty of interesting ideas on offer, you may find it hard to choose between them. Trust your intuition – it's working well. If your first impression of an enterprise dreamt up by a hare-brained colleague is not to commit yourself, don't be tempted to change your mind.

## 18 SUNDAY  ☿ *Moon Age Day 25   Moon Sign Capricorn*

The current emphasis is on creative pursuits and this is one of the things that sets this specific Sunday apart. If you are one of the many artistic Taureans, this quality in your nature is showing strongly at the moment. Use the influences well by working on some interior design, DIY or creative hobby and involve others in your schemes.

## 19 MONDAY  ☿ *Moon Age Day 26   Moon Sign Aquarius*

This is hardly the time for spending hours on jobs that demand the utmost concentration. Try to show your usual Taurean patience but at the same time be willing to go down new roads in terms of thoughts and actions. Don't be surprised if you find words of love drifting in your direction later in the day.

## 20 TUESDAY ☿ *Moon Age Day 27   Moon Sign Aquarius*

This is a good day to look at your finances as there is potential for small but regular increases if you make the right decisions. Concentrate your effort in places and situations you know and understand. You show a strong willingness to help others, especially friends you recognise to be going through a hard time at the moment.

## 21 WEDNESDAY ☿ *Moon Age Day 28   Moon Sign Pisces*

There is very likely to be love interest on the horizon for Taurus, particularly those of you who have been looking for that very special romance. Don't be too quick to jump to conclusions regarding material matters and if you are in any doubt whatsoever, opt for a patient attitude and bide your time. That's something Taurus does well.

## 22 THURSDAY ☿ *Moon Age Day 0   Moon Sign Pisces*

Keep your counsel and avoid getting carried away with issues that don't have anything directly to do with your life at present. Retain your energy for really important tasks because although you have plenty of get up and go right now, it is easily dissipated. It's quality rather than quantity that really pays off at this time.

## 23 FRIDAY ☿ *Moon Age Day 1   Moon Sign Aries*

Venus is still strong and the potential for attracting new people into your life now is very good. You will do well to overcome the shy side to your nature, and you may find this easier than usual. Most Taurus people tend to be young at heart, no matter how old they are. Go for fun, because that's the most important factor now.

## 24 SATURDAY ☿ *Moon Age Day 2   Moon Sign Aries*

Life is still looking good. You should be registering a genuinely light-hearted period, during which you find the answers you need almost without trying. If you do come up against the odd problem today, look to those closest to you – one of them is likely to be able to solve it for you. You should certainly not feel too shy or retiring to ask.

## 25 SUNDAY ☿ *Moon Age Day 3 Moon Sign Taurus*

No matter what you do today and tomorrow, don't waste the benefits of the best of all planetary influences. Both Venus and the Moon are shining favourably on you. Use your energy and optimism to tackle the projects most important to you. You should make good progress, others will support you and obstacles can be overcome.

## 26 MONDAY ☿ *Moon Age Day 4 Moon Sign Taurus*

Make sure you get up early to make the best of this auspicious day. The lunar high inspires you to be far more determined regarding plans that have been in your mind for some time. Use the confidence you feel to move things ahead. In personal relationships, you should be able to bring people round to your point of view.

## 27 TUESDAY ☿ *Moon Age Day 5 Moon Sign Taurus*

For the third day in a row, the lunar high helps you with its positive influences so it's a good time to push yourself. Taurus isn't lazy by any means but there are occasions when you find it easier not to get involved in certain situations. If you resist that temptation to stand back, you'll find it to your advantage.

## 28 WEDNESDAY ☿ *Moon Age Day 6 Moon Sign Gemini*

Making money might be something of a struggle at this stage of the week. Maybe you are not being adventurous enough or are failing to recognise a host of possibilities when they come along. It would be sensible to ask the advice of a long-time friend. Family members will offer their counsel but it might not be sound.

## 29 THURSDAY ☿ *Moon Age Day 7 Moon Sign Gemini*

Take advantage of any social and romantic offers that come your way. You should find most people are favourably disposed towards you. As there may be one or two in particular who you find very attractive, don't waste the opportunity to get acquainted. Curb a tendency to be too outspoken, especially about things you don't understand.

## 30 FRIDAY ☿ *Moon Age Day 8 Moon Sign Cancer*

Keep your ears open because you have a good chance of hearing some interesting and useful information. Assess it carefully, though, and don't take anything at face value. You need to remain determined to follow your own appointed course in life. Routines are likely to be a bit of a bind so you can improve your life by adding variety.

## 31 SATURDAY ☿ *Moon Age Day 9 Moon Sign Cancer*

The way loved ones behave should encourage you to look at life in a slightly different way and could offer room for a sort of optimism that hasn't been around in the very recent past. The smile that has been on your face throughout most of this month should be broader than ever as March draws to a close and you look forward to April.

# April

2012

## 1 SUNDAY  ☿  *Moon Age Day 10   Moon Sign Cancer*

In terms of communications at least, this is likely to be a hectic but enjoyable sort of day. You can afford to back your hunches to a great extent and should make a point of sharing your ideas – you should have plenty of them. If things begin to look too quiet, look to friends, who should be very helpful in offering some exciting alternatives.

## 2 MONDAY  ☿  *Moon Age Day 11   Moon Sign Leo*

Be careful at the beginning of this week. A professional issue could cause a rather tense atmosphere unless you take it by the scruff of the neck and deal with it immediately. You need to be very direct in all your dealings right now because hedging your bets doesn't work. Friends display some confidence in you.

## 3 TUESDAY  ☿  *Moon Age Day 12   Moon Sign Leo*

Almost anything you have planned for today will go well, just as long as you devote your usual level of effort to it. There is a strong element of luck in the influences on most aspects of your life, so this is a time to make decisions, move things forward and back your hunches all the way.

## 4 WEDNESDAY  ☿  *Moon Age Day 13   Moon Sign Virgo*

Even though you may feel slightly under stress, you can prove how reliable you are by taking complex professional issues in your stride. You can't expect everyone to agree with your point of view but if you stick to your principles you will turn out to be right in the end. You have the power to persuade and can make people listen.

# 5 THURSDAY
*Moon Age Day 14    Moon Sign Virgo*

It looks as though coming to terms with a personal issue is part of what today is about. Be confident in your dealings with others and avoid giving anyone the impression that you are not certain regarding decisions you wish to take. Friends should prove to be especially helpful at the moment and genuinely do want to lend a hand.

# 6 FRIDAY
*Moon Age Day 15    Moon Sign Libra*

Keep your counsel and avoid getting involved in arguments that belong to others. It's all too easy today to pass an opinion on almost any subject, but it won't necessarily do you any good. Be willing to leave specific subjects to people who are experts in their own field. It would be unfortunate if anyone accused you of being a know-it-all.

# 7 SATURDAY
*Moon Age Day 16    Moon Sign Libra*

A quieter phase is on the way, so you will want to use every second of today to get things done, particularly in a practical sense. By the evening, you should be able to find the time to spend with relatives, or perhaps your partner. There are some small potential financial gains, but pay attention or you could miss them.

# 8 SUNDAY
*Moon Age Day 17    Moon Sign Scorpio*

Thanks to the lunar low, some delays in favoured projects are inevitable now, which is why you have to exercise a little patience, particularly at the beginning of next week. Don't rush into anything, but use that capable Taurus brain and think things through carefully. A little preparation is worthwhile in any job you undertake today.

# 9 MONDAY
*Moon Age Day 18    Moon Sign Scorpio*

This would not be a good time to struggle against the odds. This doesn't mean that you have to give up on your best plans, merely delay them for a few hours. A little time to think won't go amiss and may even prove to be a blessing in the longer term. You are in a good position to offer some sound advice to a friend today.

## 10 TUESDAY     *Moon Age Day 19    Moon Sign Sagittarius*

Because of your willingness to give – to be supportive and to show empathy – you are generally very popular. Someone might decide that you deserve a treat because of what you have done for them and even if this is only a string of compliments it will do your ego no end of good. Romance looks good this week, so be alert to opportunities.

## 11 WEDNESDAY   *Moon Age Day 20    Moon Sign Sagittarius*

It won't be hard today to be quite opinionated. This only usually happens in the case of Taurus when you are genuinely sure of yourself but all the same you need to show your accustomed humility when you are putting your message across to others. Taurus is rarely, if ever, arrogant but it might occasionally seem that way.

## 12 THURSDAY     *Moon Age Day 21    Moon Sign Capricorn*

Now is a good time to think about expanding both your personal and professional horizons so be on the lookout for opportunities. You should feel energetic and determined so use it to present yourself in the best possible light in any situation.

## 13 FRIDAY         *Moon Age Day 22    Moon Sign Capricorn*

Don't fall into the trap of thinking Friday the thirteenth is unlucky or it could be a self-fulfilling prophecy. There are plenty of good vibes for you today, especially if you stick with co-operative efforts and teamwork activities. Taking rash decisions is never good for Taurus, so there's no reason to do so today.

## 14 SATURDAY      *Moon Age Day 23    Moon Sign Aquarius*

Keep a tight hold on your purse strings for now and don't speculate too much regarding matters you do not fully understand. Of course you could make it your business to find out what is really happening and then you would be in a better position to take a financial chance. On the whole you may decide to save money.

## 15 SUNDAY
*Moon Age Day 24    Moon Sign Aquarius*

The general pace of life could slow somewhat at the moment. The Sun is, after all, in your solar twelfth house, which often inspires a period of regeneration and a time when you will be thinking and planning towards the more positive trends to come. Take time out to be with your family and perhaps make this an old-fashioned Sunday.

## 16 MONDAY
*Moon Age Day 25    Moon Sign Aquarius*

Don't be at all surprised if there are new and interesting people entering your life around now. The Moon in particular makes you curious at the moment and you want to know what makes even strangers tick. The fact that you are interested promotes discussions and these in turn could lead to new friendships being formed.

## 17 TUESDAY
*Moon Age Day 26    Moon Sign Pisces*

Some doubts regarding a private matter need to be addressed before you can move on. If there is something you don't quite understand, there is no harm at all in asking. Something you hear at the moment may prove to be quite disappointing but it would be best not to show the fact, otherwise you could undermine your own influence.

## 18 WEDNESDAY
*Moon Age Day 27    Moon Sign Pisces*

Take full advantage of better circumstances in terms of finances and make the most of new opportunities to get ahead. Some good news should be coming in regarding money, perhaps as a result of actions you took in the past. Friends have confidences to impart and one or two of these could prove to be especially surprising.

## 19 THURSDAY
*Moon Age Day 28    Moon Sign Aries*

Don't blame others for setbacks that take place at this time. In some cases it's down to simple bad luck but there are other occasions when you need to think and act differently. People from the past are now inclined to show up in your life again and you could also be getting some interesting news from a long way off.

## 20 FRIDAY
*Moon Age Day 29    Moon Sign Aries*

Now the Sun is moving into your solar first house, which makes you more confident and which also sets the seal on plans you have been harbouring for while but which you can now put into action. People should prove to be quite supportive now and across the weekend but it's really all down to your own positive attitude.

## 21 SATURDAY
*Moon Age Day 0    Moon Sign Aries*

Today might be slightly quieter than you had been expecting but if so you are responding to the Moon, which is in your solar twelfth house. There is a good deal of planning going on inside your mind and a desire to get details straight before you push forward with new plans. Be available to offer advice to family members.

## 22 SUNDAY
*Moon Age Day 1    Moon Sign Taurus*

You can use the lunar high to make your own luck and coupled with a first house Sun, it's action stations all round. People seem to be inspired by you and no wonder. The force of your personality is evident in almost every situation and you are able to show yourself at your very best. Address practical matters where you are very efficient.

## 23 MONDAY
*Moon Age Day 2    Moon Sign Taurus*

Stronger financial potential is evident. Even if you are not actually coming into money today you have it within you to lay down plans that are going to prove very important later. In discussions you will be giving a good account of yourself, though without coming across as being in any way arrogant.

## 24 TUESDAY
*Moon Age Day 3    Moon Sign Gemini*

The good times continue. You will enjoy being the centre of attention wherever you go today. It would be a shame if the planetary aspects creating this tendency were wasted, simply because this was nothing more than a routine day. Put yourself out to make sure there are social possibilities after work and utilise them.

## 25 WEDNESDAY  *Moon Age Day 4   Moon Sign Gemini*

Keep your wits about you. A financial issue is apt to prove somewhat complicated, leading you to seek the advice of someone who is more in the know than you are. Don't avoid discussions simply because you are not in a chatty frame of mind. Things need sorting out and you won't manage that without talking.

## 26 THURSDAY  *Moon Age Day 5   Moon Sign Gemini*

It appears that having fun is likely to be your number one priority this Thursday. Although this is somewhat difficult in the midst of a busy life, this is a good time to test your ability to mix business with pleasure and to enjoy them both. Look up people who haven't been around recently and take the chance to have a chat.

## 27 FRIDAY  *Moon Age Day 6   Moon Sign Cancer*

The emphasis on the fun side of life continues and it is possible that you find it difficult to take certain matters seriously. It might be worth your while to pretend that you do, though this is mainly to keep the good opinion of those around you. Give yourself a genuine pat on the back for a recent success that is likely to lead to others.

## 28 SATURDAY  *Moon Age Day 7   Moon Sign Cancer*

The good times continue. You are in a very strong position to call the shots where future plans are concerned. What matters is that you are doing your homework, which others may not manage so well. This will mean that your point of view is reasoned and difficult to fault. Your business decisions should prove extremely shrewd.

## 29 SUNDAY  *Moon Age Day 8   Moon Sign Leo*

It's plain to see that this is the time to put fresh ideas to the test. You won't want to feel in any way fettered and show a strong determination to do what pleases you. Since you are presently so charming, it is unlikely that anyone would deliberately stand in your way. Don't be afraid of some limited but well thought out speculation.

# 30 MONDAY

*Moon Age Day 9   Moon Sign Leo*

To feel at your best today, seek out varied and different company. This is not a day to think security and comfort, under these auspices you should be putting yourself to the test in a physical sense. Make sure you remember birthdays in the family and amongst your friends. This is a good emailing day so get writing.

# May

2012

## 1 TUESDAY
*Moon Age Day 10    Moon Sign Virgo*

More significant advancement is now likely, probably because of all the effort you have put in recently. This doesn't necessarily refer to work. If you are a member of any particular organisation, you could be invited to take on a position of responsibility. In one way or another, the world is looking at you with confidence.

## 2 WEDNESDAY
*Moon Age Day 11    Moon Sign Virgo*

A short interlude shows that today is definitely one of those times during which you get out of life almost exactly what you put into it. If you want to be lethargic, situations won't demand much of you, but you won't make the gains either. Better by far to go for gold and then to revel in the attention that comes your way.

## 3 THURSDAY
*Moon Age Day 12    Moon Sign Virgo*

Your ability to command attention and impress others can be put to the test today. With plenty going for you in a general sense and material situations still looking good, it's time to put in the effort. Although not everyone appears to have your best interests at heart, when it matters most friends come up trumps.

## 4 FRIDAY
*Moon Age Day 13    Moon Sign Libra*

It looks as though you won't have the hours for personal indulgences today and will be tied up, probably most of the time, with one issue or another. If you can break away, do your best to foster some personal desire or aspiration. The more you feel you are moving forward, the greater is the incentive for a positive period.

## 5 SATURDAY
*Moon Age Day 14    Moon Sign Libra*

It appears that material issues are uppermost in your mind at present and you need to face some of these head-on and early in the day. In friendships you are positive and aspiring, though it is in terms of love and romance that you tend to have the best of all worlds today. People simply want to love you and to be kind.

## 6 SUNDAY
*Moon Age Day 15    Moon Sign Scorpio*

Unexpected obstacles come along today, thanks to the lunar low. However, you should be able to make the best of them if you are not afraid to rely on people whom you know have natural good luck. On a personal level, today ought to prove both interesting and stimulating so don't get too bogged down with difficulties to notice.

## 7 MONDAY
*Moon Age Day 16    Moon Sign Scorpio*

Venus has moved into your solar second house and this can give you opportunities to increase your finances significantly across the coming weeks. You need to take the right actions now in order to make the most of these positive trends and that will involve looking at new money-making schemes, plus a high degree of co-operation.

## 8 TUESDAY
*Moon Age Day 17    Moon Sign Sagittarius*

With the Sun in your solar first house you are filled with energy so use it to make this one of the most productive periods of the year so far. You should feel fairly good about life because this is definitely your time and your optimism knows no bounds. Others may remark about how good you look at present – enjoy the compliments.

## 9 WEDNESDAY
*Moon Age Day 18    Moon Sign Sagittarius*

This is a week for putting the finishing touches to something and for concentrating on new plans that are just starting to mature. Put yourself in the way of conversations that could be pleasant and informed. That should be easy as you are good to know and popular. Romantic options should be open to you too, so be alert to opportunities.

## 10 THURSDAY     *Moon Age Day 19     Moon Sign Capricorn*

The time is right for you to pursue personal freedom and you are likely to get the best outcome if you push your luck a little when it comes to new attachments. The last thing you want is to be restricted in any way or to feel that you cannot follow your chosen direction. Try to avoid being too stubborn if you don't get your own way.

## 11 FRIDAY     *Moon Age Day 20     Moon Sign Capricorn*

You are likely to be quite subjective in your evaluations of life. In some ways you could be so keen to make the right impression that you forget what it is you were supposed to be doing. Avoid spending too much time standing in front of the mirror and get out there and do things. Instincts are going to be your best guide now.

## 12 SATURDAY     *Moon Age Day 21     Moon Sign Aquarius*

You have the capacity this weekend to occupy a high-profile position, most probably amongst your friends but possibly at work if you have to toil away on a Saturday. Whatever you are doing at the moment is undertaken with both a smile and a flourish. This really is Taurus at its best and you'll have plenty of energy to cope with life.

## 13 SUNDAY     *Moon Age Day 22     Moon Sign Aquarius*

Social-group activities are the best area of your life to focus on, whether you are mixing with lifelong friends or people you have only just met, as you are sure to continue to make a favourable impression. If you have been a little jumpy regarding the state of your finances, you should now be able to simplify matters.

## 14 MONDAY     *Moon Age Day 23     Moon Sign Pisces*

Lots of travel is possible this week and although many of the journeys you take could be local in nature, they are far-reaching in scope and potential. This is the start of a week that brings a mixed bag of possibilities though almost everything should be geared towards your long-term success and your own personal growth.

## 15 TUESDAY          *Moon Age Day 24    Moon Sign Pisces*

If you make any investments during this part of the week they are likely to be well thought out and quite sound. Although you can be quite excitable in some respects, make sure you are not too rash – unlikely but worth guarding against. There is time and incentive to check things out before you commit yourself to any financial deal.

## 16 WEDNESDAY          *Moon Age Day 25    Moon Sign Aries*

You probably have a great urge for competition, so grasp any opportunities to test yourself against others and you will have the best chance of coming out on top. Mars is the only fly in the ointment and its position could indicate a slight tendency to strains and sprains so if the contest is physical, make sure you prepare well.

## 17 THURSDAY          *Moon Age Day 26    Moon Sign Aries*

Try to organise and simplify your surroundings if you can. Life may be getting a bit cluttered and this is the first time this year when the fact has really occurred to you. Taurus hates to throw things out but there are times when you simply need more space in those wardrobes. Be ruthless and clear away what is holding you back.

## 18 FRIDAY          *Moon Age Day 27    Moon Sign Aries*

With the Moon in your solar twelfth house you are likely to feel quite thoughtful today. Enjoy it, and don't try to push things as much as you have been doing recently. Someone you have only just met could have a cracking idea and you will want to be involved, but avoid committing yourself today. Wait until tomorrow at least.

## 19 SATURDAY          *Moon Age Day 28    Moon Sign Taurus*

The lunar high arrives and brings with it the most potent part of the month. If there is anything you want to do, now is the time to get on with it. Don't take no for an answer and if necessary see to all the details yourself. You will be happier that way in any case because for the moment you know you have the best ideas.

## 20 SUNDAY
*Moon Age Day 0    Moon Sign Taurus*

An early start will allow you to reap all the benefits of the planetary influences so you should have lots done by lunchtime and be quite happy with your progress. On the social front, be quick to take any opportunity – this is the sort of Sunday when you are likely to have fun whatever you choose to do.

## 21 MONDAY
*Moon Age Day 1    Moon Sign Gemini*

Your strong point is your versatility and with Mercury now in your solar first house there is plenty to do and lots of energy to get through it all. You may have the chance to meet new people today – take it, as they will become much more important to your life in the future. Enjoy feeling very optimistic about all sorts of things.

## 22 TUESDAY
*Moon Age Day 2    Moon Sign Gemini*

This is a time for consolidation and a period during which you will get on well if you tackle one thing at a time. Your levels of concentration are high, and you are most likely to be satisfied with progress if you focus on specific objectives. Other people could be moving from one thing to another; ignore them and remain steadfast.

## 23 WEDNESDAY
*Moon Age Day 3    Moon Sign Gemini*

The focus of this time is money and possessions so turn your attention to your financial situation. Taurus needs to feel secure and not wondering how things will go in the weeks and months ahead. Anything you can do to increase your sense of security is worth a second look now – and maybe a third one too.

## 24 THURSDAY
*Moon Age Day 4    Moon Sign Cancer*

This is a good time to be getting your message across so pay attention to any matters that test your communication skills. If you speak from a position of confidence and authority, most people will take your word for almost anything. Don't allow yourself to be over-modest, as you often do. Allow this popularity to feed your confidence.

## 25 FRIDAY

*Moon Age Day 5   Moon Sign Cancer*

This is a good time to build on recent beginnings and to show the world just how much you know. It seems as though a great deal of learning has gone into the last couple of years and it is now beginning to pay definite dividends. Creative potential is especially good today so you can start new interests with enthusiasm.

## 26 SATURDAY

*Moon Age Day 6   Moon Sign Leo*

The effect you have on the world at large is now more marked than you might have expected. Enjoy the fact that you are even making an impression on people you didn't think had much time for you. At home, you are friendly to everyone and should be very open-minded when it comes to the suggestions of younger people.

## 27 SUNDAY

*Moon Age Day 7   Moon Sign Leo*

Your domestic life could begin to get rather more demanding than of late. It is very important to you to run a happy and a peaceful home and that is certainly possible under present trends. At the same time there are likely to be family members who are in something of a muddle and who could benefit from your organisational skills.

## 28 MONDAY

*Moon Age Day 8   Moon Sign Leo*

For those of you who are looking, there could be new possibilities appearing on the romantic horizon. You need to be mixing with people who are as open and optimistic as you are and to stay away from negative types or those who seem to have an end gain in everything they do. A good friend is in need of your sound advice.

## 29 TUESDAY

*Moon Age Day 9   Moon Sign Virgo*

Investments or purchases are likely right now and you will be keeping your eyes open for that very special bargain that is likely to be coming your way between now and the weekend. You can probably afford to spoil yourself a little and should not be quite as careful with money as often proves to be the case for Taurus.

## 30 WEDNESDAY $\qquad$ *Moon Age Day 10 $\quad$ Moon Sign Virgo*

When you encounter any sort of obstacle right now you will be inclined to stand back and look at it before trying to proceed. This may sometimes take a while but the effort pays off. Certainly you should avoid banging your head against the same brick wall time and again because the result will only be a very sore head!

## 31 THURSDAY $\qquad$ *Moon Age Day 11 $\quad$ Moon Sign Libra*

It is likely that today may at first seem to be one of the less successful days of May, although in reality what you do has repercussions of a very positive sort that will not become obvious until later on. It isn't like you to be impatient but with the lunar low arriving in a day or two you could easily be fidgety and lacking in tolerance.

## June

2012

# 1 FRIDAY
*Moon Age Day 12   Moon Sign Libra*

The first day of June looks potentially interesting and also possibly exciting for many Taurus subjects. All the same, don't take on anything today that will involve you in hard work across the weekend. You need to look to a quiet Saturday and Sunday if you possibly can, so slow things down and prepare to take some rest.

# 2 SATURDAY
*Moon Age Day 13   Moon Sign Scorpio*

Some frustration is possible today, mainly because you can't do exactly what you want at the moment you wish to do it. Taurus is quite capable of extreme relaxation and you should take the advantage to ruminate for a couple of days. If you do get out and about, make sure it is to somewhere beautiful and inspiring.

# 3 SUNDAY
*Moon Age Day 14   Moon Sign Scorpio*

The lunar low is still around so you won't have the same level of determination and vitality that was obvious throughout most of May. On the other side of the coin, your powers of concentration are particularly good. Anything that makes you look hard and think deeply is favoured, though probably on your own rather than in a group.

# 4 MONDAY
*Moon Age Day 15   Moon Sign Sagittarius*

Your approach to life is unique this week, but almost certainly successful. Don't be put off if people see you as being slightly quirky, they still find you entertaining. Don't spend all of Monday on practical tasks but rather leave some hours during which you can please yourself, whilst offering others a good time too.

## 5 TUESDAY     *Moon Age Day 16*    *Moon Sign Sagittarius*

Look out because specific people will be making quite significant demands of you today. If this turns out to be the case, you will simply have to refuse some requests, particularly on those occasions when you are sure you are being taken for a mug. Stick up for yourself and you will be respected.

## 6 WEDNESDAY    *Moon Age Day 17*    *Moon Sign Capricorn*

Inconsequential issues can be distracting but in the main you appear to be getting on rather well in life. Romance offers diversions for some Taureans today, particularly those who are young or young at heart. Social diversions will be welcome and a good night out with friends would suit you down to the ground.

## 7 THURSDAY     *Moon Age Day 18*    *Moon Sign Capricorn*

It's quite possible that some hopeful news is on the way, in some instances from far-off places. Look at mail carefully. Communication is the key to success as far as Taurus is concerned now and you might even find yourself caught up in email relationships or spending long periods of time on the telephone.

## 8 FRIDAY     *Moon Age Day 19*    *Moon Sign Aquarius*

You should be enjoying a fairly successful run if you are a working Bull. If not, there are gains to be made at home and for all those born under this zodiac sign there is a strong chance of travel. Fresh starts are increasingly likely when it comes to out-of-work activities and especially those undertaken with friends.

## 9 SATURDAY     *Moon Age Day 20*    *Moon Sign Aquarius*

It would appear that you are working better in groups about this time. That hasn't always been the case earlier in June but now you find it easier to come to terms with team decisions and you can contribute to a much more progressive communal phase. Run with it and you will find it both enjoyable and rewarding.

# 10 SUNDAY
*Moon Age Day 21    Moon Sign Pisces*

All sorts of minor pressures and demands could keep you on the go today. There's no let-up in the general desire to have fun and no matter what your age you'll enjoy yourself if you participate. Try something new and don't be beaten before you've made the effort. It's likely that you will surprise yourself before the end of the day.

# 11 MONDAY
*Moon Age Day 22    Moon Sign Pisces*

Using pressure tactics or bullying when trying to get your own way with others won't work all that well for the moment. Better by far to talk reasonably and to offer a degree of friendly advice. Such a way of behaving will get you much further than being a bulldozer. Look out for romantic potential later.

# 12 TUESDAY
*Moon Age Day 23    Moon Sign Pisces*

Confidence should be slightly increased today, but you still feel somewhat contemplative and less inclined to take any sort of chance than was the case even last week. Rules and regulations can be something of a bind and leave you feeling rather hemmed in. Break through red tape when possible and keep a positive attitude.

# 13 WEDNESDAY
*Moon Age Day 24    Moon Sign Aries*

Keep your eyes open because good news could be coming in from a number of different directions, some of which prove to be quite surprising. You take this in your stride and at the same time you seek change and diversity in your life as a whole. Don't be too surprised if you are being singled out for special treatment.

# 14 THURSDAY
*Moon Age Day 25    Moon Sign Aries*

It is almost certain that only a little effort on your part will be needed to make most matters go your way today. If there are celebrations amongst your family or friends, take every chance to join in and have fun. You have a fairly carefree attitude to life at present and can certainly enjoy all that romance offers.

## 15 FRIDAY
*Moon Age Day 26   Moon Sign Taurus*

You shouldn't have to work as hard as usual to achieve your personal and professional aims. If those around you appear to be conspiring to make your life more comfortable, that's all to your advantage. The lunar influence can make you feel far more confident of your own capabilities than usual – don't waste that feeling.

## 16 SATURDAY
*Moon Age Day 27   Moon Sign Taurus*

With the lunar high around it won't be too difficult to get your own way now, even with people who are tougher to crack than nuts. The fact is that you are seen as being very likeable and a good deal more flexible than is occasionally the case for Taurus. Acting on impulse is not really you, but it does seem to work at present.

## 17 SUNDAY
*Moon Age Day 28   Moon Sign Taurus*

You will be pleased to hear that you won't have to look too hard for good fortune today because the Moon should ensure it comes your way of its own accord. Although you are lucky today, you are not invulnerable. Take time in your day to spend at least a few moments thinking about your personal security.

## 18 MONDAY
*Moon Age Day 29   Moon Sign Gemini*

It's a mixed bag today. Although many of your personal ambitions are now clearly on course, don't overstep the mark and expect too much, either of others or yourself. You need to tread carefully where finances are concerned and not push other people into taking financial risks that they might find considerably unnerving.

## 19 TUESDAY
*Moon Age Day 0   Moon Sign Gemini*

Keep moving forward and look out for a peak in terms of your professional life. If you are between jobs, or looking for something new, this would be a good time to keep your eyes open. Try to say the right things and be prepared to get involved in timely chats with people who are in the know – they could be useful to you.

## 20 WEDNESDAY           *Moon Age Day 1    Moon Sign Cancer*

It is fairly clear that you can benefit from someone's advice but this will not be the case unless you listen first. There is a slight tendency for you to plough your own furrow, irrespective of circumstances. Be open in your attitude and don't dismiss alternative strategies simply because they did not occur to you first.

## 21 THURSDAY           *Moon Age Day 2    Moon Sign Cancer*

Things are looking quite good and the tempo of life may be increasing, bringing you a greater sense of purpose and personal satisfaction. Mercury is presently in a good position to offer you excellent ways of communicating your ideas to others. It might occur to you today that a greater degree of co-operation would be sensible.

## 22 FRIDAY           *Moon Age Day 3    Moon Sign Cancer*

Be prepared for a boost coming along as far as your social life is concerned. If you get together with others, you can make for an interesting time, once the concerns of the material world have been dealt with. You could also notice an upturn in general fortune and financial strength. This should be beginning at any time now.

## 23 SATURDAY           *Moon Age Day 4    Moon Sign Leo*

This is a good time for you to impress others and you should find you don't have to try very hard. However, compromise is a word you do need to keep in mind and there is no gain at all now from refusing to adapt, even though that's what you are inclined to do. Be thoughtful, though, as impulsive actions are less likely to bring rewards.

## 24 SUNDAY           *Moon Age Day 5    Moon Sign Leo*

It appears that your partner could now play a more dominant role in your life but only because that is the way you want the situation to be. In other spheres, you need to look very carefully at suggestions that are being made which somehow have a bearing on your working circumstances. Perhaps negotiation is necessary.

## 25 MONDAY
*Moon Age Day 6    Moon Sign Virgo*

This continues to be a bonus period for personal relationships and for love especially, so make sure you show your partner or sweetheart how you feel about them. Aim high when it comes to personal objectives and don't be put off by one or two people who are naturally quite pessimistic and who don't know your capabilities.

## 26 TUESDAY
*Moon Age Day 7    Moon Sign Virgo*

Keep talking! Your powers of communication especially are in the ascendant today and you seem to have what it takes to get your message across to others clearly. If there is a particularly big task before you, the best approach today may be to nibble away at the edges of it, or perhaps to seek the help of a good friend.

## 27 WEDNESDAY
*Moon Age Day 8    Moon Sign Libra*

Although you could be in two minds regarding practical decisions, in the end your Earth-sign common sense can tell you what to do. Do you take the advice of others or simply forge ahead under your own steam? The truth is that you are going to rely almost solely on logic at present, whether you realise the fact or not.

## 28 THURSDAY
*Moon Age Day 9    Moon Sign Libra*

Thursday could be a good time to put financial plans into action, most likely in conjunction with either business or personal partners. As far as romance is concerned, you should be looking out today for someone who is clearly making overtures. Whether you are interested or not remains to be seen, but you should be flattered.

## 29 FRIDAY
*Moon Age Day 10    Moon Sign Scorpio*

Spirits and optimism could be flagging around this time. The lunar low isn't going to bring much in the way of bad luck but it will find you floundering on occasions to find the right approach to any given situation. Confidence will return soon enough. For the moment it may be advantageous if you decide to remain fairly quiet.

# 30 SATURDAY

*Moon Age Day 11   Moon Sign Scorpio*

It looks as though you will want some moments of reflection today. That's quite understandable with the lunar low around and it offers you the chance to plan somewhat more carefully than has been possible for the last few days. Be careful not to get stuck in a rut – why not plan something good for tomorrow?

# ⑧
# *July*
2012

## 1 SUNDAY
*Moon Age Day 12    Moon Sign Sagittarius*

Be prepared for a new and busy phase that begins around now. You ought to be feeling quite bright and breezy and there will be no shortage of incentives to get ahead. Romance isn't immune to the present trends, as you are about to discover. You still have admirers, even if some of them have to virtually shout for you to realise.

## 2 MONDAY
*Moon Age Day 13    Moon Sign Sagittarius*

Planetary aspects remain good and there appears to be plenty of challenging cut and thrust to the day. This is particularly true with regard to relationships. Some people who cross your path will be entirely helpful but you can't expect this to be the case universally. Take the ups and downs in your stride – you can learn from them both.

## 3 TUESDAY
*Moon Age Day 14    Moon Sign Capricorn*

This could so easily be one of the best days of the month to experience and encourage personal freedom within yourself. Although you are still putting yourself out for the sake of others, it is the way you go about it that counts. Being restricted in any way could be almost physically painful right now. You need to feel unfettered.

## 4 WEDNESDAY
*Moon Age Day 15    Moon Sign Capricorn*

For the first time in ages your love life tends to have its slight problems right now. For starters you are not so willing or able to see the other person's point of view. Extra flexibility is going to be required and you must do everything you can to examine points that are put to you before you react strongly against them.

## 5 THURSDAY          *Moon Age Day 16    Moon Sign Capricorn*

It is true that certain people can cause you small problems, though only if you are mixing with the wrong sort of individuals. Your deep intuition should tell you when this is the case. The answer is simple: stay away from them. Concentrate instead on people with whom you have plenty in common and who make you laugh.

## 6 FRIDAY          *Moon Age Day 17    Moon Sign Aquarius*

As is often the case for you, getting your own way with others now is largely a matter of charm, of which you have in great abundance at present. Confidence is growing rapidly, particularly in terms of your forward planning at work. The weather outside should be reasonably good now and you would benefit from some fresh air.

## 7 SATURDAY          *Moon Age Day 18    Moon Sign Aquarius*

Look to all aspects of travel to bring pleasure into your life this weekend. Outdoors, or at home, you know what you want from life so go after it with the energy of this planetary alignment. What really sets the seal on a good weekend is the fact that you now find yourself willing to leave behind some recent difficulties.

## 8 SUNDAY          *Moon Age Day 19    Moon Sign Pisces*

Take some time out because relaxing at home now could ease some of the pressure you might have been registering at work across the last week. It is more than likely that a family member has some interesting advice for you today. Instead of only half listening, spend an hour or two going through situations with them.

## 9 MONDAY          *Moon Age Day 20    Moon Sign Pisces*

There is a chance that things could be less than perfect at work today. Don't overburden yourself with responsibility but try to allow others to do some of the decision making. The fact is that you are probably not in the mood and you need to do something different in order to recharge your batteries.

## 10 TUESDAY
*Moon Age Day 21    Moon Sign Aries*

Don't allow petty issues to overwhelm you. The Moon has now moved into your solar twelfth house. This makes you more contemplative and less inclined to be pushy or determined. It won't be long before the lunar high comes along but in the meantime you could do worse than to allow things to ride for a while.

## 11 WEDNESDAY
*Moon Age Day 22    Moon Sign Aries*

With the Sun in your solar third house you are slightly restless and anxious to get things going. All the same, today is better for planning than doing and you need to talk things over with both colleagues and friends before you act. The personal side of your life is likely to be quite settled but do look out for exciting potential.

## 12 THURSDAY
*Moon Age Day 23    Moon Sign Taurus*

Many Taureans will now be feeling more confident and will be wanting to get on with life in as big a way as proves to be possible. The lunar high increases your potential for luck and allows you to go for gold, especially in work-based issues. At the same time you are extremely communicative and anxious to talk to almost anyone.

## 13 FRIDAY
*Moon Age Day 24    Moon Sign Taurus*

It's Friday the thirteenth but that fact is hardly likely to bother you at all with the lunar high in place. If you are willing to get the very best out of life and create new chances, the planets are on your side. You should expect more success and will approach the weekend with greater optimism than you have had so far this month.

## 14 SATURDAY
*Moon Age Day 25    Moon Sign Taurus*

An active and very energetic weekend is forecast. You begin Saturday with the lunar high still in place and will be anxious to prove that you can not only work hard but that you can play hard too. Make the most of the summer weather and perhaps think about taking an outing of some sort – in the company of people you care for.

## 15 SUNDAY    ☿    *Moon Age Day 26    Moon Sign Gemini*

If you are at work today, you need to follow your instincts. If not, do something different and keep up the variety in your life. With the Sun in its present position just about your best gift is that you can talk and talk – use it to your advantage. The things you have to say seem important to others and conversations bring new ideas.

## 16 MONDAY    ☿    *Moon Age Day 27    Moon Sign Gemini*

This ought to be a favourable time for new ideas and the beginning of a new working week should find you right on the ball and anxious to make headway with long-term and short-term plans. There is a slight chance that you will come up against some sort of opposition, most likely from jealous types, but try to ignore it.

## 17 TUESDAY    ☿    *Moon Age Day 28    Moon Sign Gemini*

Communication matters continue to thrive and intuitive ideas can be brought forward and discussed with a host of different people. If there are any contracts that need signing, now is the time to think about putting pen to paper. You remain extremely astute and will not fail to read the small print – no matter how detailed it is.

## 18 WEDNESDAY    ☿    *Moon Age Day 29    Moon Sign Cancer*

At work, be careful that you are not coming across as being bossy and slightly overbearing. Be aware of the risk and it will be easy to redress by remembering that you need to keep listening as well as talking for communication to work. You may not mean to be pushy but you could offend others if that's what they perceive.

## 19 THURSDAY    ☿    *Moon Age Day 0    Moon Sign Cancer*

In terms of your career this might be a somewhat challenging day. You need to think carefully about long-term motives and to ask yourself if some of the things you are trying to do are strictly necessary. Times could be changing and a new emphasis is possible for the Taurus life, which might mean letting go of something.

117

## 20 FRIDAY ☿ *Moon Age Day 1   Moon Sign Leo*

All sorts of new ideas could be of interest to you now and some of them need to be put into practice. In a few days the Sun moves on in your chart and although it brings many positive prospects, it will be slightly more restricting when it comes to you showing your power in the outside world, so now is the time to act.

## 21 SATURDAY ☿ *Moon Age Day 2   Moon Sign Leo*

Mercury is now in your solar fourth house and this is going to be very useful when it comes to the domestic side of life. Look out for gains coming your way that have something to do with property and with the people you live amongst. Much of your energy is gradually being turned in the direction of your home and family.

## 22 SUNDAY ☿ *Moon Age Day 3   Moon Sign Virgo*

Today could be a day filled with more genuine fun than has been the case for a short while. Use this interlude to your advantage and, without trying to achieve anything in particular, simply have a good time. Those closest to you should be quite happy to join in and you can make the most of a summer Sunday.

## 23 MONDAY ☿ *Moon Age Day 4   Moon Sign Virgo*

You have a strong thirst for fresh experiences now. Seeking out change and variety in your life is likely to be extremely important and there are very few difficult trends to deal with right now. Although you are still good at problem solving, you might have to seek out an expert during today or tomorrow to ask their advice.

## 24 TUESDAY ☿ *Moon Age Day 5   Moon Sign Libra*

You should perhaps take a fairly cautious approach to money matters just now, but the same cannot be said in the realms of romance, where trends are favourable. You instinctively shower your loved one with so many compliments that they will be happy to follow your lead and will be putty in your hands.

## 25 WEDNESDAY ☿     *Moon Age Day 6    Moon Sign Libra*

Intuition is now the key. Some of the problems you come across today simply cannot be overcome using pure logic. Although logic is usually your first resort, you can be quite intuitive, particularly at the moment. Some lateral thinking could benefit you and you should avoid taking the most obvious approach if it just doesn't feel right.

## 26 THURSDAY ☿     *Moon Age Day 7    Moon Sign Libra*

It's worth paying attention today because the most casual of meetings could turn into something much more interesting. Although there are one or two people around who are not all that trustworthy, seeing through such individuals isn't at all difficult. The most appealing thing about today is the sheer volume of work you get through.

## 27 FRIDAY ☿     *Moon Age Day 8    Moon Sign Scorpio*

Whilst the lunar low is around it might be sensible to allow your partner or another family member to deal with some of the major issues on the home front. Although you can hold your own at work, there may not be the same feeling of progress that has been around for quite a few days now. Home should be a welcome retreat.

## 28 SATURDAY ☿     *Moon Age Day 9    Moon Sign Scorpio*

You can't really expect to be number one today and if you realise why, then disappointments are less likely. This might be a good time for shopping, as long as spending is moderate, and you can also organise things very well, particularly in terms of working practices. Major successes are not all that likely today.

## 29 SUNDAY ☿     *Moon Age Day 10    Moon Sign Sagittarius*

This is Sunday and it would be best to opt for some light relief. There are substantial gains to be made where friendship is concerned, so look out for opportunities. Social situations could also lead you to discover ways to get ahead both personally and financially. Today may start out slowly but will gain momentum later on.

## 30 MONDAY ☿ *Moon Age Day 11    Moon Sign Sagittarius*

As a new week begins there is good assistance for practical projects, as long as you are willing to go out and look for it. It is quite likely that some of your present ideas have plenty of potential, although unless you seek some help, you may never know. Watch out for some possible surprises where your love life is concerned.

## 31 TUESDAY ☿ *Moon Age Day 12    Moon Sign Capricorn*

Treat today with a light touch and focus on almost anything that is on your personal agenda, particularly in the first part of the day. Later on, you are likely to feel more contemplative and may choose to spend some time on your own, or at least in small groups. Home seems a good place to be this month.

⑧

# *August*

2012

## 1 WEDNESDAY ☿ *Moon Age Day 13 Moon Sign Capricorn*

It would be sensible to avoid allowing yourself to be dominated by emotional impulses, particularly since many of them are unnecessary. You need to free yourself from old habits and especially ones that you know are bad for you. If you adopt a forward-looking attitude later in the day, you'll feel much more contented.

## 2 THURSDAY ☿ *Moon Age Day 14 Moon Sign Aquarius*

Look to your instincts because you'll create confusion if you put your faith in the wrong people today. It might be better to follow your own conscience in most matters and to stay away from deliberately provocative types. None of this prevents you from enjoying a generally happy and quite useful sort of Thursday.

## 3 FRIDAY ☿ *Moon Age Day 15 Moon Sign Aquarius*

You can push ahead in specific directions with confidence today as you will feel sure you know what you are doing. Any small disappointments early in the day are likely to be swamped by much better trends later on. Even if you are busy, make time to spend with the people you care about.

## 4 SATURDAY ☿ *Moon Age Day 16 Moon Sign Pisces*

You continue to take life in your stride and are unlikely to be fazed by much on what proves to be a fairly sensible sort of Saturday for Taurus. Sensible is fine, but it doesn't create excitement, and you need some of that too. Try not to be willing to settle for second best but push forward progressively.

## 5 SUNDAY ☿ *Moon Age Day 17 Moon Sign Pisces*

With the Sun now so firmly in your solar fourth house there is no doubt at all that you are committed to family and to your home. Domestic issues come thick and fast and tend to be the centre of your thinking, especially on a Sunday. You may choose to spend time in your garden or somewhere beautiful quite close to home.

## 6 MONDAY ☿ *Moon Age Day 18 Moon Sign Aries*

Issues from the past are inclined to arise again now and you may need to consider your present actions in light of what you did before. It is very important at present to be honest with yourself and not to ignore what you know is the truth. If you remain straightforward, this could be the start of a solid and a very positive sort of week.

## 7 TUESDAY ☿ *Moon Age Day 19 Moon Sign Aries*

Do your best today, but don't be surprised if what you accomplish falls short of your expectations. This comes from the position of the Moon in your chart, which also makes you quite contemplative and inclined to worry a little about details. Be patient. By Thursday, you should be able to set your sights on new goals.

## 8 WEDNESDAY ☿ *Moon Age Day 20 Moon Sign Aries*

As if you hadn't noticed, it's high summer now and you ought to be thinking about all those things that need doing around your home whilst the weather is good. Family members will be needing your special touch today and might be calling a little too freely upon your resources. A gentle reminder could be in order.

## 9 THURSDAY *Moon Age Day 21 Moon Sign Taurus*

You can certainly afford to be enterprising and enthusiastic today, as the lunar high brings new incentives and plenty of energy into your life. While others are jumping around from foot to foot wondering what you do, you are accomplishing a great deal. Turn towards romance later in the day and make a stupendous impression.

# 10 FRIDAY
*Moon Age Day 22   Moon Sign Taurus*

Now is definitely the time to rely heavily on your intuition and also to push your luck more than you might have chosen to do earlier in the week. You create a very good impression of yourself, no matter what you decide to do and it is likely that your level of good luck is much higher than it has been so far during August.

# 11 SATURDAY
*Moon Age Day 23   Moon Sign Gemini*

Whilst decisiveness and quick thinking are usually a bonus, your move towards efficiency in practical matters might be somewhat thwarted today by the actions of those around you. Take a slower and more certain approach because that is the way Taurus usually achieves its most cherished objectives.

# 12 SUNDAY
*Moon Age Day 24   Moon Sign Gemini*

Your best moments in life today are likely to come as a result of home and family. With less to do in a truly practical sense you can spend a few hours enjoying the time of year and also revelling in the company of those who are closest to you. This should also be a very warm and secure interlude in terms of your romantic life.

# 13 MONDAY
*Moon Age Day 25   Moon Sign Gemini*

Venus is in your third house now, so you should be especially good at expressing yourself in terms of love. You won't take kindly to any sort of discord right now so you will want to do all you can to pour oil on troubled water, particularly at home. Routines that you have been shunning might now seem more comfortable.

# 14 TUESDAY
*Moon Age Day 26   Moon Sign Cancer*

There's no doubt about it. With Mars in its present position you will not take at all kindly to rules and regulations being imposed upon you. There is something of the rebel about you just now and you will quite happily fight hard against what you see as being either bullying or coercion. Use the trends wisely to avoid being too bombastic.

## 15 WEDNESDAY          *Moon Age Day 27    Moon Sign Cancer*

Right now you definitely benefit from change and variety in your life. Don't settle for second best in anything and be prepared to put in that extra bit of effort that can make all the difference. You will be especially inclined towards travel whilst the Moon occupies its present position and holidays are definitely on the cards for many.

## 16 THURSDAY          *Moon Age Day 28    Moon Sign Leo*

It looks as though you will feel quite sentimental at the moment. With the Sun still in your solar fourth house you will also be turning your attention towards the domestic side of your life and towards the people who are the most important to you. Take the opportunity to re-establish links with old friends, maybe after a very long break.

## 17 FRIDAY          *Moon Age Day 0    Moon Sign Leo*

Get into the habit of planning ahead and then you won't have to rush yourself or decide on your agenda at the last moment. Taurus doesn't like to be pushed into anything and you are in danger of digging your heels in rather than doing anything you are not sure about. This could be against your best interests so try to be flexible.

## 18 SATURDAY          *Moon Age Day 1    Moon Sign Leo*

Today could see you quite assertive and anxious to let people know your likes and dislikes. Too much attention to detail isn't to be recommended on this summer Saturday and you would be better off keeping life casual and spontaneous if at all possible. Family members might be quite demanding later in the day.

## 19 SUNDAY          *Moon Age Day 2    Moon Sign Virgo*

You don't like getting your hands dirty at the best of times and especially not now. Taurus is a cultured zodiac sign and not one that responds well to untidy or cluttered surroundings. Today you could feel this more acutely than usual so it's a good day to spend at least part of today tidying up – and encouraging others to do the same.

124

## 20 MONDAY                    *Moon Age Day 3    Moon Sign Virgo*

There's change in the air as the week begins. You may want to rethink your strategies somewhat, which should mean that you end the day in a stronger position than you began it. Rules and regulations could get in the way of the sort of progress you envisage but if you deal with matters as and when necessary, you'll still get ahead.

## 21 TUESDAY                   *Moon Age Day 4    Moon Sign Libra*

Any issues that crop up between yourself and your partner need resolving as quickly as possible. There is a sense of urgency in your life generally and it's clear that you are keen to get on and achieve. Not everyone will be equally helpful at present so turn your attention to the people closest to you as they can offer useful, practical help.

## 22 WEDNESDAY                 *Moon Age Day 5    Moon Sign Libra*

Creative potential is especially good today so take the chance to make more of your home surroundings. Keeping busy won't be a problem at any stage and this is a good time to be planning for an action-packed time ahead. You'll certainly have the confidence to develop plans and projects, just be careful you don't take on too much.

## 23 THURSDAY                  *Moon Age Day 6    Moon Sign Scorpio*

Some delays are more or less inevitable today and that could mean frustration if you are on the move. Try not to let it stress you out. People with your zodiac sign have the potential to make the best of whatever situation they find themselves in and showing your philosophical qualities will pay off today.

## 24 FRIDAY                    *Moon Age Day 7    Moon Sign Scorpio*

Important decisions need to be left alone for the moment. The lunar low is a period you can enjoy most by being relaxed and willing to go with the flow. Travel could be uppermost in your mind once again so give in to the temptation of seeking out somewhere beautiful to spend a few hours, even if you don't go very far afield.

## 25 SATURDAY      *Moon Age Day 8    Moon Sign Sagittarius*

Now it looks as though you can gain from productive talks, most likely with people you already know quite well. This would be an ideal phase to start a new regime, so, for example, if you are a smoker, why not think about kicking the habit now? Planetary trends favour change and you are more in the mood to contemplate them.

## 26 SUNDAY      *Moon Age Day 9    Moon Sign Sagittarius*

The urge for personal freedom is clear and strong at the moment. The quality of your life should be good and with the lunar low now well out of the way, minor frustrations ought to be a thing of the past. In both work and play you exhibit a genuine love for life and a desire to get ahead, no matter what the obstacles. This is a time to go for it!

## 27 MONDAY      *Moon Age Day 10    Moon Sign Capricorn*

There is a balanced feel today, with things going along happily. Your natural charm means there is little likelihood of arguments with others, especially as you are patient and willing to accept that your point of view, though unique, isn't the only one worth considering. Small financial gains are indicated later so watch for opportunities.

## 28 TUESDAY      *Moon Age Day 11    Moon Sign Capricorn*

All forms of communication are well favoured and you are particularly willing to see the other person's point of view so talks at home could help to put certain situations in a better light. If you use the opportunity well, you will be able to overturn any negative views and make people look at you in a newer and more positive way.

## 29 WEDNESDAY      *Moon Age Day 12    Moon Sign Aquarius*

Taking the initiative could lead to great successes on the professional front. On the personal side, it would be best not to embark on too rigid a regime of dieting, or giving up nights out just now. With so much going your way, you should be out there enjoying yourself. You can avoid excesses without missing out on the fun.

## 30 THURSDAY     *Moon Age Day 13    Moon Sign Aquarius*

It looks as though you are now willing to stimulate the competitive instincts that you naturally possess but don't always use. People won't get away with trying to fool you today and if you enjoy puzzles of almost any sort, today feels like a good day to enter that competition! Try to make an opportunity to spend time in the fresh summer air.

## 31 FRIDAY     *Moon Age Day 14    Moon Sign Pisces*

Look out for what could be a slightly difficult day emotionally. You need to be sure that you understand what others are saying, and particularly your partner. As long as you are willing to talk things through steadily, all should be well. What you shouldn't do is fly off the handle without being fully in possession of the facts.

# ⑧ September 2012

## 1 SATURDAY
*Moon Age Day 15    Moon Sign Pisces*

It should be plain that your versatility is what counts at the moment. You can turn your hand to almost anything, and what is more you enjoy yourself while you are at it. This would be a wonderful time to take a late holiday or even a short break. Keep plugging away with regard to objectives you know to be important.

## 2 SUNDAY
*Moon Age Day 16    Moon Sign Pisces*

Along comes Sunday and friendly co-operation is what sets today apart. You can make gains through patience, perseverance and through being in the right place at the best possible time. Intuition works strongly, leading you to all sorts of conclusions that might astound others. In a social sense, variety is now the spice of life.

## 3 MONDAY
*Moon Age Day 17    Moon Sign Aries*

It is probably not advisable to believe everything you hear today because there are likely to be a few people around who have some sort of interest in pulling the wool over your eyes. You might have to let go of something that has been important to you in the distant past but which now has more or less run its course.

## 4 TUESDAY
*Moon Age Day 18    Moon Sign Aries*

Mercury in your solar fifth house suggests wit, cleverness and an active sense of humour. This is a good time to use your skills to get what you want from other people. If you apply gentle persuasion, you are likely to be successful. Don't push too hard, though, as arguments are less likely to go your way and should be avoided.

128

## 5 WEDNESDAY      *Moon Age Day 19    Moon Sign Taurus*

You can make good things happen at this time as you will be very positive in your outlook and eager to make things happen. You can afford to push your luck somewhat as people around you will be seeing you for the intelligent person you are. Don't allow today to be all about work because there is scope for enjoying yourself.

## 6 THURSDAY      *Moon Age Day 20    Moon Sign Taurus*

The message today is: don't hold back. You should be promoting yourself as your ability to resolve problems of other people's making is particularly strong. Embark on some troubleshooting and you may be surprised at how easily things fall into place. Plus you will do it with confidence and be appreciated by those you help out.

## 7 FRIDAY      *Moon Age Day 21    Moon Sign Taurus*

Although the lunar high is still around during the first part of the day, in the main you will be responding more to the planet Mars right now and that tends to make you slightly more argumentative and certainly not likely to back down if you feel you are being crossed in some way. Don't overdo the Taurean stubbornness.

## 8 SATURDAY      *Moon Age Day 22    Moon Sign Gemini*

These are good vibes for the weekend as you'll know how to keep a conversation going because your sense of humour is so well honed. If you have to work, try to avoid working all the time, even if you are doing something you don't dislike. You need a few hours to relax and spend some quality time with your partner and family.

## 9 SUNDAY      *Moon Age Day 23    Moon Sign Gemini*

Your sunny disposition is still on show, as is your robust constitution and your desire to push the bounds of the credible. As a result a more adventurous Bull is on display and you might decide to try something you have shied away from in the past. Stay away from anything that is definitely dangerous but you can push yourself a little.

# 10 MONDAY
*Moon Age Day 24    Moon Sign Cancer*

This is a time during which your powers of persuasion are extremely good. Mentally speaking you are right on the ball so you have what it takes to turn many situations to your advantage. Not everyone is going to consider you flavour of the month but a fair proportion of people will and it is these individuals who count today.

# 11 TUESDAY
*Moon Age Day 25    Moon Sign Cancer*

Mars remains in your solar seventh house, which is not an entirely favourable position for you. It is inclined to make you consider that your own point of view is the most important one, which could blind you to other possibilities and alienate you slightly from some other people. Be aware of the tendency so you can nip it in the bud.

# 12 WEDNESDAY
*Moon Age Day 26    Moon Sign Cancer*

This is a good time to be embarking on keeping things tidy, or improving your general décor at home. If you don't fancy any creative DIY, try to put yourself in the most luxurious surroundings you can. It's possible that family members may cause you unusual concern but you are more than capable of dealing with it.

# 13 THURSDAY
*Moon Age Day 27    Moon Sign Leo*

The focus remains on the domestic front because in addition to Venus, the Moon is also in your solar fourth house today and tomorrow. A nostalgic trend is also likely to show and you might be tempted to spend an unreasonable amount of time thinking about what was and what might have been instead of looking forwards productively.

# 14 FRIDAY
*Moon Age Day 28    Moon Sign Leo*

If you remain optimistic and cheerful, you are likely to win many admirers and this, in turn, will help you to succeed because others are so willing to pitch in on your behalf. You should be feeling fairly good about yourself generally, so don't be too cautious. You can afford to push the boundaries, especially socially.

# 15 SATURDAY          *Moon Age Day 29   Moon Sign Virgo*

At home you should find getting along with others to be easy enough. Your partner will be doing all they can to make you happy, efforts you are only too willing to return, leading to an easy-going and conciliatory atmosphere all round. Make at least part of the weekend a time for travelling, even if it is only short distances.

# 16 SUNDAY          *Moon Age Day 0   Moon Sign Virgo*

It looks as though you are now rather eager to be the centre of attention and you can expect a favourable response under the present planetary line-up. You can put these influences to good use both socially and at work in whatever opportunities arise. Your partner and family may have high expectations but you can rise to the challenge.

# 17 MONDAY          *Moon Age Day 1   Moon Sign Libra*

It looks as though you will remain confident and energetic, and it is mostly thanks to the present position of the Sun in your solar chart. You will enjoy friendly competition and although the competitive edge is quite evident, it doesn't force you to become aggressive or confrontational so you are likely to get your way.

# 18 TUESDAY          *Moon Age Day 2   Moon Sign Libra*

When it comes to personal relationships and general attachments, now is the time to make decisions and take action because today people around you may be happy to put themselves out on your behalf. But the lunar low is on the way and by the end of the day, you could find they are less amenable and significant progress becomes difficult.

# 19 WEDNESDAY          *Moon Age Day 3   Moon Sign Scorpio*

Just because things are not going exactly as you would wish, there's no need to give in to feeling grumpy. Admit you are in a bad mood and it's no-one's fault, then you are likely to find the clouds lifting and other people will stop avoiding you.

## 20 THURSDAY          *Moon Age Day 4    Moon Sign Scorpio*

You might encounter arguments and dissension around you today, though it has to be said that you are not exactly as optimistic yourself as has been the case recently. It's probably for the best if you keep a low profile; that way you can avoid confrontation. The mood won't last long so just ride it out.

## 21 FRIDAY          *Moon Age Day 5    Moon Sign Sagittarius*

The place you learn things most quickly at this time will be at work. Not only can you acquire new skills if you put your mind to it, you can also learn useful information if you just keep your ears open. You are likely to feel much more cheerful now the lunar low is receding, so you can enjoy a return to your usual equanimity.

## 22 SATURDAY          *Moon Age Day 6    Moon Sign Sagittarius*

Some partnerships could now seem fraught with emotional baggage, much of which needs to be sorted out and left behind. If a good heart-to-heart can achieve this, then the effort will have been very worthwhile. What you don't need now is arguments. You won't start them but don't be sucked in as you may not win them either.

## 23 SUNDAY          *Moon Age Day 7    Moon Sign Capricorn*

Travel arrangements may have to be changed, in some cases at the last moment. Don't assume this will necessarily be a bad thing because something quite surprising and delightful might arise as a result. What you need today is flexibility and a willingness to follow circumstances, rather than feeling you can predict everything yourself.

## 24 MONDAY          *Moon Age Day 8    Moon Sign Capricorn*

Things should still be going well at home, which is probably why you spend as much time there at the moment as you can. With Mars in its present position there could be a few jitters with regard to public appearances, especially if you are expected to speak to a large group of people. Don't worry, you will do fine.

## 25 TUESDAY    *Moon Age Day 9    Moon Sign Aquarius*

You certainly have the ability to command attention today and should be making sure you turn heads wherever you go. With some positive planetary positions around and others developing, don't waste your potential to progress projects and make things happen. Your positive energy should make you popular with those around you.

## 26 WEDNESDAY    *Moon Age Day 10    Moon Sign Aquarius*

It is at this time that doing your own thing seems most important. There are moments now when you simply don't want to follow instructions, especially when they come from people who don't know what they are talking about. The sarcastic side of your nature could just show and you may need to bite your tongue.

## 27 THURSDAY    *Moon Age Day 11    Moon Sign Aquarius*

A significant focus on domestic issues and home life in general should make for a reasonably comfortable sort of day. Your ideas are not quite so grandiose as they have been across the last two or three weeks, but you may have a chance to demonstrate how gentle and caring you are. A couple of calculated gambles could pay off today.

## 28 FRIDAY    *Moon Age Day 12    Moon Sign Pisces*

An instinctive understanding of situations lies at the heart of your efforts today. Don't allow yourself to be bullied into doing anything that goes against the grain; let your conscience rule your decisions. For the romantically inclined, this is a day to take your chances. Don't rush to resolve personal issues; allow them to take their course.

## 29 SATURDAY    *Moon Age Day 13    Moon Sign Pisces*

There are some potentially interesting encounters around during the weekend, though not if you insist on staying behind closed doors. Now you need to spread your wings and there are people around you who will be only too willing to take a trip somewhere special with you. Make a real fuss of your partner this weekend.

133

# 30 SUNDAY                    *Moon Age Day 14    Moon Sign Aries*

It appears that you will have certain duties to fulfil and not all of
them will be equally enjoyable. However, these should not take the
edge off your ability to enjoy this Sunday. Although the inclination
to travel has been strong within you for some weeks now, today's
tendency is more a stay-at-home one.

# ♊ October

2012

## 1 MONDAY
*Moon Age Day 15    Moon Sign Aries*

The week starts out well and it looks as though this is going to be a good time for broadening your horizons in some way. Take every opportunity to try something new and don't be held back simply because others don't take the same point of view. Avoid family rows by getting out of the house if it proves to be necessary.

## 2 TUESDAY
*Moon Age Day 16    Moon Sign Taurus*

With the lunar high comes a certainty in your mind that you are generally going in the right direction. Take advantage of every opportunity to make a good impression and be prepared to push your luck as much as you can. There is room for variation in your schedule today, which the position of the Moon supports.

## 3 WEDNESDAY
*Moon Age Day 17    Moon Sign Taurus*

Now filled with optimism and high spirits, you need to make today special in some way. Giving others a helping hand might not be a bad start and you should also be thinking in terms of changes you can make in and around your home. Best of all, you feel the need to get out and party – if you can find someone willing to join in.

## 4 THURSDAY
*Moon Age Day 18    Moon Sign Gemini*

The pursuit of outdoor interests is likely to prove a fascination to many Taurus people now. The present position of the Sun makes you more intrepid than usual and also fills you with wanderlust and a sense of wonder regarding the world beyond your door. If you start a new regime now, don't go too mad.

135

# 5 FRIDAY
*Moon Age Day 19    Moon Sign Gemini*

You can afford to indulge your ego today and allow others to make a fuss of you. Family members and friends are genuinely impressed by your accomplishments so don't be over-modest. Of course, you will be aware that you still have a long way to go towards your objectives but for now enjoy the fact that people notice your efforts.

# 6 SATURDAY
*Moon Age Day 20    Moon Sign Gemini*

Extended talks and general negotiations seem to be the order of the day. Some of these will prove to be very useful, whilst others don't offer quite the rewards you may have been expecting. Treat each situation on its own merits and don't be too alarmed if some people appear to be quite disruptive. Things can be sorted out.

# 7 SUNDAY
*Moon Age Day 21    Moon Sign Cancer*

This should be a promising sort of day. You can put your versatile powers to good use today and get even more from your involvement with the world as a whole. Don't expect to agree with everyone, or that they will necessarily believe everything that you say. All the same, arguments won't help so settle for frank discussion.

# 8 MONDAY
*Moon Age Day 22    Moon Sign Cancer*

Whether you are at work or play today, you tend to surround yourself with some interesting people and you should be having a generally good time. Your outgoing and happy nature is definitely on display and that means people generally will be doing all they can for you. This ought to be a rewarding interlude.

# 9 TUESDAY
*Moon Age Day 23    Moon Sign Cancer*

Ideas, plans and thoughts should flow smoothly between yourself and others, so this would be an excellent time for working in partnerships or for getting involved in new ventures with colleagues. Friends also have some good ideas and you will probably want to be involved in these from the start.

# 10 WEDNESDAY

*Moon Age Day 24    Moon Sign Leo*

Today you remain serious about your ambitions and your goals in life – but not so serious that you put any sort of damper on the good social trends that are surrounding you. Prospects for romance and affairs of the heart are good today, offering you good romantic prospects and some heart-warming times if you act swiftly.

# 11 THURSDAY

*Moon Age Day 25    Moon Sign Leo*

There seems to be so much happening around you at the moment, especially in your love life, that you can become dizzy with the potential. Don't make the mistake of not acting just because there's so much choice. New friendships are possible and you may spot a chance to rekindle an old flame that has burned lower recently.

# 12 FRIDAY

*Moon Age Day 26    Moon Sign Virgo*

At this time you are likely to be feeling especially creative and you can best satisfy your personal goals by trying new things. You will want to be surrounded by order and, if possible, luxury – something that is always close to the Taurean heart. Work with your family or partner to make some design changes at home.

# 13 SATURDAY

*Moon Age Day 27    Moon Sign Virgo*

Always a hard worker, now you are more than willing to put in the time and effort to promote your own well-being and that of those you care for. Once again you should find that romance is high on your agenda and also that of your lover. If you have just embarked on a new relationship, your input should be rewarded.

# 14 SUNDAY

*Moon Age Day 28    Moon Sign Libra*

Communication with just about anyone should be working well and you won't have too much trouble making yourself fully understood – even to people who are not generally easy to deal with. Give yourself the time necessary to get your head round a rearrangement or a major new item at home and, in the meantime, be patient.

## 15 MONDAY    *Moon Age Day 0    Moon Sign Libra*

Your concern now turns towards orderliness in the workplace. It's clear that at the moment you want things to be just so and you'll need to exercise patience with anyone who seems to be throwing a spanner in the works. In a social sense, your tidy mind can be put to good use in sorting out the mess created by a friend.

## 16 TUESDAY    *Moon Age Day 1    Moon Sign Libra*

This is the last day before the lunar low that will slow down your progress, so it would be sensible to get things in order and to be prepared to let others do some of the work over the next few days. Your sympathetic side is favoured now, so keep in touch with distant friends and look for ways to help people you don't even know.

## 17 WEDNESDAY    *Moon Age Day 2    Moon Sign Scorpio*

Many of your plans might not seem to be workable over the next couple of days and you'll find it difficult to overcome negative thinking because of the lunar low. If you can't rise to that challenge, try to let things ride if you can and don't take any prohibitive action. By the end of the week, things should become clearer.

## 18 THURSDAY    *Moon Age Day 3    Moon Sign Scorpio*

It could seem that no matter how hard you try, you are getting nowhere fast. This is because you continue to knock your head against a brick wall. Stop trying to achieve the impossible. Stand back and observe and you'll regain your objectivity. The more you relax, the better you will deal with these negative astrological circumstances.

## 19 FRIDAY    *Moon Age Day 4    Moon Sign Sagittarius*

In business and financial matters in particular, you will need to take care that everything you are dealing with is well organised and above board. If you do that, even the most apparently disruptive circumstances should turn out for the best in the end. Try to save major decisions until later in the day.

## 20 SATURDAY     *Moon Age Day 5     Moon Sign Sagittarius*

There are new opportunities to broaden your horizons coming from the Moon and also your friend Venus. There is likely to be a little good fortune coming your way and you need to be on the ball because this could come from an unexpected direction. It is very important to act and react fairly quickly right now.

## 21 SUNDAY     *Moon Age Day 6     Moon Sign Capricorn*

You tend to meet obstacles with patience and a good sense of humour, which is probably more than can be said for certain other people in your vicinity. Much of the time you have the feeling that you have to rely on yourself and that those around you are not working efficiently or sensibly, but try to continue to offer them your support.

## 22 MONDAY     *Moon Age Day 7     Moon Sign Capricorn*

Look out for a change in direction at work, with new responsibilities likely to come your way and with a host of different opportunities starting to present themselves. In most situations you show yourself to be active and enterprising, leaving nobody in any doubt that you know what you are doing and are worth following.

## 23 TUESDAY     *Moon Age Day 8     Moon Sign Aquarius*

Look out for the chance to make new friends, as well as strengthen love ties. Not everyone is going to be on your side in practical matters but you should be able to use your persuasive nature to get them on side. Don't be deflected from your objective on the rare occasion when you can't bring others round to your point of view.

## 24 WEDNESDAY     *Moon Age Day 9     Moon Sign Aquarius*

The Sun is now in your solar seventh house and this strengthens friendships and also romantic relationships. Taurus has been on a real winner for most of this year when it comes to attachments and you should still be taking advantage of your popularity. There is a strong possibility that you will be travelling now or in the near future.

## 25 THURSDAY
*Moon Age Day 10    Moon Sign Pisces*

If there are changes coming along in your working environment you need to take these on board and even welcome them if you can. Taurus, like all Earth signs, tends to stick to what it knows but this can be a negative reaction sometimes. You need to be progressive and to encompass new technologies and improved techniques.

## 26 FRIDAY
*Moon Age Day 11    Moon Sign Pisces*

Mercury now assists in bringing a boost to most relationships. If things have been flagging somewhat in a particular attachment or friendship, look out for ways to pep things up and to make life more interesting. Be careful what you eat at the moment because stomach upsets are slightly more likely than usual.

## 27 SATURDAY
*Moon Age Day 12    Moon Sign Aries*

Finding yourself influenced by irrational thoughts is part of the legacy of the Moon's position around this time. It would be best not to dwell on things and to keep yourself active over the weekend, though with the lunar influence coming from the twelfth house you are bound to be slightly contemplative and not so quick on the uptake.

## 28 SUNDAY
*Moon Age Day 13    Moon Sign Aries*

Slight disruptions to daily routines come courtesy of the planet Mars, though it is by no means certain that these will prove to be negative. Sometimes you need to be jogged into looking at life in an alternative way and this seems to be what is happening at the moment. Take some time out to meditate a little today.

## 29 MONDAY
*Moon Age Day 14    Moon Sign Aries*

This ought to be a good start to the week, particularly because by tomorrow the lunar high will be with you. For now you need to look ahead and to plan what your actions are likely to be. You love to know where you are going and why, though there are some occasions when it is simply best to follow good fortune wherever it goes.

# 30 TUESDAY *Moon Age Day 15   Moon Sign Taurus*

Now you can move up a few steps in life, just by being in the right place and by taking the correct actions. Decisions are likely to be instinctive while the lunar high is in place and those you make are likely to be good ones. Keep a positive view of the future and make things turn out the way you would wish them to be.

# 31 WEDNESDAY *Moon Age Day 16   Moon Sign Taurus*

Your career life in particular should be enriching today, though it has to be said that with your present attitude you can gain pleasure and success from all sorts of situations. When you are not at work you need to be associating with people who not only make you happy but who also stimulate you to forge new paths.

# ♏ ⑧ November 2012

## 1 THURSDAY
*Moon Age Day 17   Moon Sign Gemini*

The first day of November should find you to be fair-minded and very balanced in your opinions. The truly charitable side of your nature is clearly on display and you will be in a frame of mind to do just about anything you can to help out people in trouble. You may want to offer practical support, or simply a listening ear.

## 2 FRIDAY
*Moon Age Day 18   Moon Sign Gemini*

Aim to maintain a positive attitude today, which will make others instinctively trust and like you. Popularity is not hard for the average Taurus individual to find, even if you don't always have the confidence to believe it. When you doubt yourself, try to recall the sense of self-confidence you have experienced today.

## 3 SATURDAY
*Moon Age Day 19   Moon Sign Gemini*

You are so active this weekend that you might have to spread yourself more thinly than you would wish. As a result it could feel to certain friends or family members that you don't have sufficient time for them. You need to offer reassurance, especially to your partner. Meanwhile, a modicum of good luck is likely to come your way.

## 4 SUNDAY
*Moon Age Day 20   Moon Sign Cancer*

It looks as though your tendency right now is not so much to work round things but to ride over the top of them. This comes thanks to the position of Mars, which is now in your solar eighth house. It is important to get where you want to be but the route you take is also significant. Don't be a bulldozer today because others won't like it.

## 5 MONDAY                    *Moon Age Day 21    Moon Sign Cancer*

You could now be sensing some fairly inevitable changes in your life and it would be good to know that it was you deciding what should alter. You need to think quite deeply about certain aspects and also to get some good advice from people in the know. November can be quite reactive for you and very eventful.

## 6 TUESDAY                    *Moon Age Day 22    Moon Sign Leo*

You can be a definite agent for change today if you apply yourself properly. You are a natural reformer and can do things now that will improve the lot of others, as well as having a significant bearing on your own life. Where money is concerned, you may have been fairly conservative recently but could afford to take some risks now.

## 7 WEDNESDAY   ☿    *Moon Age Day 23    Moon Sign Leo*

With Mars in your solar eighth house, the winds of change are blowing around you. Sweep away some emotional cobwebs and you will free yourself to move forward towards new incentives and maybe even new friendships or attachments. There could be something of the reformer about you as you seek to help others to have a better life.

## 8 THURSDAY   ☿    *Moon Age Day 24    Moon Sign Leo*

The accent today is more or less totally on fun and pleasure, even if you have to go to work. Look for the fun in any situation and involve others in your zany schemes. Taurus is light-hearted and fun-loving in almost everything and it will be especially difficult for you to take any aspect of life totally seriously today – so why bother?

## 9 FRIDAY   ☿    *Moon Age Day 25    Moon Sign Virgo*

This would be a very fortunate time for business discussions and for making alterations to the way you do things in a practical sense. It could be that you now recognise you have been chasing some sort of rainbow recently. This leads to more concerted action and a definite change of emphasis now and over the weekend.

# 10 SATURDAY ☿ *Moon Age Day 26  Moon Sign Virgo*

Your main focus now remains on doing what you can to help others, though your attitude isn't entirely charitable because you are doing yourself some good at the same time. Have some fun during the weekend and get together with like-minded people whenever you can. It would also be good to find time to show how romantic you are.

# 11 SUNDAY ☿ *Moon Age Day 27  Moon Sign Libra*

Mars remains in your solar eighth house and this can sometimes make you slightly ruthless in your determination to get your own way. Fortunately most, if not all, of what you want is for the good of everyone, so your positive attitude is not used selfishly. All the same, there may be times when you need to explain yourself.

# 12 MONDAY ☿ *Moon Age Day 28  Moon Sign Libra*

This is the last day before the lunar low arrives for November and it might turn out to be one of the most progressive days of the month so far. This will make it all the more disconcerting when the brakes are applied. For this reason you should consciously slow things down towards the end of the day and prepare for a quieter patch.

# 13 TUESDAY ☿ *Moon Age Day 0  Moon Sign Scorpio*

It would not be in the least surprising to find that you feel somewhat lacklustre today or that you cannot get yourself motivated in the way you wish. Let others do some of the hard work while you sit back and supervise. You are still making your own choices and as far as your determination is concerned, little seems to have changed.

# 14 WEDNESDAY ☿ *Moon Age Day 1  Moon Sign Scorpio*

It is likely that you will feel pulled in different directions today. Your loyalty lies in more than one place, so deciding who you should please may not be easy. While the Moon is in Scorpio it is probably best not to try. You are not quite as ingenious now as you have been, or as you will be in the days ahead. Delay the decision if you can.

144

## 15 THURSDAY ☿ *Moon Age Day 2* *Moon Sign Sagittarius*

Your generally contented outlook on life makes you popular with just about everyone today and allows you to push the boundaries of possibility when it comes to getting those around you to do what you want. A little cheek can go a long way and you could end up very surprised at just how much you can influence people.

## 16 FRIDAY ☿ *Moon Age Day 3* *Moon Sign Sagittarius*

Today is a day for looking for new opportunities and showing the world just how much common sense you can demonstrate. Getting other people's backing for your schemes should not be too much of a challenge, while your resolve will remain firm when dealing with authority figures. There's no sign of your occasional shyness.

## 17 SATURDAY ☿ *Moon Age Day 4* *Moon Sign Capricorn*

Your natural detective instincts come to the fore as you seek to ferret out the truth. The weekend could be interesting and useful when it comes to discovering what is really going on around you and there could be some surprises regarding the behaviour of a friend or family member. In the main you should be fairly happy and contented.

## 18 SUNDAY ☿ *Moon Age Day 5* *Moon Sign Capricorn*

Creativity can be enhanced now and, whether you are at home or at work, your focus should be on making things look and feel beautiful. Enlisting the support of family members and especially your romantic partner should be fairly easy and together you can enjoy whatever you are doing. A trip away from home seems likely.

## 19 MONDAY ☿ *Moon Age Day 6* *Moon Sign Aquarius*

Show some caution now. A specific scheme that you have been hatching recently might be found to contain certain glitches. It would be a shame to come so far and then to abandon something that might work very well. Instead, see what you can do in order to make a few running repairs. Friendship is still extremely important.

# 20 TUESDAY ☿ *Moon Age Day 7  Moon Sign Aquarius*

Taurus is on form and the spotlight is on personal matters, so it's a period that is excellent for focusing on your closest attachments. Where there has been a little discord, you should be able to restore reconciliation and warmth, even thought it may not be your attitude that has changed but the ideas and opinions of others.

# 21 WEDNESDAY ☿ *Moon Age Day 8  Moon Sign Pisces*

Things are looking good and there is a strong social boost to the day, together with new incentives that might look particularly exciting. Think about social outings to places of entertainment and when it comes to having a good time in the company of friends, don't hold back. Almost everyone wants to be your friend now.

# 22 THURSDAY ☿ *Moon Age Day 9  Moon Sign Pisces*

Things just seem to get better. Friendship and group encounters generally appear to have a great deal going for them right now. What they provide is a platform to boost your confidence, maybe at a time when your self-esteem has been at a slightly low ebb. Make time to socialise, particularly by the evening.

# 23 FRIDAY ☿ *Moon Age Day 10  Moon Sign Pisces*

Certain compromises are going to be necessary now if you want to get on with others as well as you know you can. Review your efforts in a professional sense and if any sort of extra responsibility is offered, don't turn it down without careful consideration. You need to start planning the social aspects of the weekend right now.

# 24 SATURDAY ☿ *Moon Age Day 11  Moon Sign Aries*

It looks as though consolidation is the key to getting on well now. Instead of firing off with new ideas, look carefully at the ones you have been addressing recently. It might take only a very small amount of effort to put the seal on weeks or months of work. Be on the look-out for the possibility of new friendships.

## 25 SUNDAY ☿ *Moon Age Day 12 Moon Sign Aries*

Time spent alone today won't be wasted. The Moon is in your solar twelfth house and the more positive push, coming from the direction of the lunar high, is just around the corner. Although you won't exactly retreat from situations that require a more dynamic approach, there's no harm in being more pensive for today.

## 26 MONDAY ☿ *Moon Age Day 13 Moon Sign Taurus*

Look around carefully because a word in the right ear can work virtual miracles at present. Throw yourself in to whatever you do today, which will feel particularly good after a few days when not everything has worked out exactly as you wished. Aim to make progress in matters of the heart and really enjoy yourself today.

## 27 TUESDAY ☿ *Moon Age Day 14 Moon Sign Taurus*

You will be able to take full advantage of almost any situation now. With friends willing to do what they can to assist, your best option is to embark on a distinctly social day, with plenty of enjoyment possible and some financial gains also in evidence. Don't be tardy when it comes to expressing an opinion.

## 28 WEDNESDAY *Moon Age Day 15 Moon Sign Taurus*

Life continues to be hectic today and also brings with it significant interest in new and exciting projects. Keep abreast of news and views in your area and think about giving more to your local community. There could be some small financial gains on the way but you need to keep on top of where money is really coming from.

## 29 THURSDAY *Moon Age Day 16 Moon Sign Gemini*

Everyday issues should keep you happily on the go today. Don't expect a startling series of events, but things should be reasonably enjoyable. Try not to allow yourself to get bogged down in details that don't really matter or worrying about people who are doing fine. Make sure you maintain your efforts on a recent project.

# 30 FRIDAY
*Moon Age Day 17    Moon Sign Gemini*

Romance is the order of the day and you will be in a great mood to hand out all those little compliments that can make other people feel so good. It isn't only personal attachments that should be going well because you seem to be getting on well with just about everyone. There is no room for arguments today so be conciliatory.

# ⑧ December 2012

## 1 SATURDAY
*Moon Age Day 18    Moon Sign Cancer*

Along comes the weekend and your luck with money certainly doesn't appear to have run out. Venus ought to be reasonably supportive in financial terms and there are also possible gains on the work front. Some relationships need a new approach, which necessitates a change of attitude on your part and some reorganisation.

## 2 SUNDAY
*Moon Age Day 19    Moon Sign Cancer*

Though optimism and positive thinking go a long way at this time, you'll also need to apply practical common sense and ability. Try not to allow your judgements to be swayed too much and when you are forced to take actions that you know are quite surprising to others, explain yourself fully first.

## 3 MONDAY
*Moon Age Day 20    Moon Sign Cancer*

You may now be in discussion regarding some emotionally-based matter and it's a fact that much of what is happening at the start of this week will be associated with your home. Things can be solved quite easily just as long as you are willing to talk and with Mercury in its present position that should not be a problem.

## 4 TUESDAY
*Moon Age Day 21    Moon Sign Leo*

Attend to unfinished business early today and then you will have plenty of time to look at all the new opportunities that are surrounding you. At work you may tire of being told what to do and could want to break out of restrictions you see as being pointless. Meanwhile there are many new social opportunities coming along.

## 5 WEDNESDAY     *Moon Age Day 22    Moon Sign Leo*

You may need to beware today because you are likely to be more outspoken than is good for you and less willing than usual to keep quiet for the sake of peace and quiet. Taurus can be quite stubborn on occasions and this could be one of them. You may need to bite your lip – or have to exercise a degree of humility later.

## 6 THURSDAY     *Moon Age Day 23    Moon Sign Virgo*

It seems as though you will be looking for a more advantageous social position as you entertain others and keep people smiling throughout most of today. You generally have an interesting story to tell and you won't have to try too hard to maintain your standing as the centre of attention. Your personal life should take a turn for the better.

## 7 FRIDAY     *Moon Age Day 24    Moon Sign Virgo*

Look out for entertaining experiences that come one after another under present astrological trends. Christmas isn't too far away, though the realisation may be only just dawning on you. Make sure you know what gifts people want and maybe do something about getting hold of some of them as soon as you can.

## 8 SATURDAY     *Moon Age Day 25    Moon Sign Libra*

Self-determination on your part paves the way towards achieving personal goals around this time. Put your best foot forward, particularly in practical matters, and show the world at large just how capable you can be. Later in the day you may find that the romantic responses coming your way are not quite what you expected.

## 9 SUNDAY     *Moon Age Day 26    Moon Sign Libra*

You are likely to be turning your attention to situations that are no longer relevant, and it's a good time to do some clearing out – whether that's of your cupboards or your emotional baggage. Taurus, being an Earth sign, is inclined to hang on to things rather too much but there are times when a clearout is in order and this is one of them.

## 10 MONDAY    *Moon Age Day 27   Moon Sign Scorpio*

It would not be surprising if you experienced some difficulties in emotional relationships just now. But nothing that happens at present is likely to shake your equilibrium too much as your naturally forgiving nature is still very much in evidence. It might be best take a little rest and not to push yourself too hard.

## 11 TUESDAY    *Moon Age Day 28   Moon Sign Scorpio*

It could feel as if you are not totally in charge of your own destiny at this stage of the week and that can make you rather uncertain and somewhat hesitant. Don't worry, because these trends are very temporary. By tomorrow you should be right back on form but for the moment you may have to rely more heavily on other people.

## 12 WEDNESDAY    *Moon Age Day 0   Moon Sign Sagittarius*

Once again you tend to feel very sociable and easy-going as the worst excesses of the lunar low disappear completely. With Christmas firmly in your sights, you will be socialising a lot more than might have been the case earlier in the month and it also looks as though you will be quite busy in every practical sense at the moment.

## 13 THURSDAY    *Moon Age Day 1   Moon Sign Sagittarius*

Formalities and tact don't mean quite as much to you today as would generally be the case. The fact is that you are going to be rather more direct and to the point than usual. This may be no bad thing, especially if someone has been taking you for granted. Your reactions today should make others brush up their act.

## 14 FRIDAY    *Moon Age Day 2   Moon Sign Capricorn*

Today's personal news may put you nicely in touch with the wider world and this in turn reminds you of concerns that exist a long way from your own front door. You become a more charitable animal at this time of year and will want to do what you can to help those who are less well off than you are. Taurus is always a 'caring' sign.

## 15 SATURDAY · *Moon Age Day 3 · Moon Sign Capricorn*

The focus at the moment is likely to be on relationships and some of these look stronger than ever as the joy and nostalgia associated with the Christmas period begin to take hold. Mercury is presently in your solar eighth house and this could incline you to make specific changes to some of your relationships.

## 16 SUNDAY · *Moon Age Day 4 · Moon Sign Aquarius*

Today could be a good time to focus on the very practical aspects of life. Roll up your sleeves and get cracking today, sorting out all those issues that have been left on the shelf for a while. It's part of clearing the decks ahead of the holidays and it is something that Taurus is inclined to do regularly at this time of year.

## 17 MONDAY · *Moon Age Day 5 · Moon Sign Aquarius*

The week might start slowly and it is possible that you will now feel that not enough is happening in your vicinity. If this does turn out to be the case, you need to put in that extra bit of effort that can make all the difference later on. There are slightly more active times on the way but they take a while to get going.

## 18 TUESDAY · *Moon Age Day 6 · Moon Sign Aquarius*

You tend to be quite outspoken now so if you are involved in discussions it is possible that you will have to guard your tongue. Speaking out of turn now could bring problems further down the road. The right sort of circumstances to allow material progress may not be present at first but they do develop later.

## 19 WEDNESDAY · *Moon Age Day 7 · Moon Sign Pisces*

You may be in two minds about certain issues today and especially those connected with work. If this turns out to be the case, you really need to use your intuition, which is working well at this time. Avoid getting into any sort of logjam by varying your routines and also by thinking about things in different ways.

## 20 THURSDAY
*Moon Age Day 8    Moon Sign Pisces*

What an ideal time this is to be out there in the social mainstream of life. Parties and gatherings of any sort appeal to you because you are likely to be the life and soul of any function. However, be careful how much you eat and drink because otherwise you may end up regretting your tendency towards excess.

## 21 FRIDAY
*Moon Age Day 9    Moon Sign Aries*

You should allow others to take some of the strain now, leaving you to watch and supervise. Luckily for you, colleagues are quite likely to fall in with this arrangement, perhaps affording you a little relaxation. Don't be in the least surprised if someone has a few very positive comments to make about you.

## 22 SATURDAY
*Moon Age Day 10    Moon Sign Aries*

It looks as though challenges will come along at this time, and most of them will be welcome, since they offer you the chance to show exactly what you are made of. The objections that others might make about your life may only serve to show where their own faults lie. For this reason alone, it isn't worth rising to the bait.

## 23 SUNDAY
*Moon Age Day 11    Moon Sign Taurus*

Changing solar influences come along now that stimulate your natural curiosity regarding the world and the way it runs. It would be sensible to communicate your thoughts to professionals or people you respect. With communication well favoured, even the most casual remarks you make are likely to be taken on board.

## 24 MONDAY
*Moon Age Day 12    Moon Sign Taurus*

Christmas Eve puts a spring in your step and a smile firmly on your face. The fact is that with the lunar high about, you are the life and soul of any party. Friends and relatives alike seem to be doing all they can to make you happy now, though most of the effort is clearly coming from your direction.

## 25 TUESDAY          *Moon Age Day 13    Moon Sign Taurus*

It cannot get much better than having the lunar high present during Christmas itself. You should be full of energy and anxious to get as much out of the day as you possibly can – by putting plenty in. People will warm to your infectious humour and to the fact that you put yourself out so much on their behalf. A really good day.

## 26 WEDNESDAY          *Moon Age Day 14    Moon Sign Gemini*

Things remain generally positive. You score many points in social situations and particularly so if you are away from home and enjoying the hospitality of others. Try to pitch in and not be critical about the way those around you arrange their functions. Too much fussing won't get you anywhere today so try to stay relaxed.

## 27 THURSDAY          *Moon Age Day 15    Moon Sign Gemini*

Take a break. Whatever you decide to take on board today, keep it simple. Relatives and friends alike will do all they can to lighten your load and since you have probably been on the go since before Christmas Eve, why not allow others to spoil you? In matters of the heart, you should be on the receiving end of significant compliments.

## 28 FRIDAY          *Moon Age Day 16    Moon Sign Cancer*

Since you need to express yourself fully now, there's a chance you will be so busy talking that you will overlook a few fairly important details. This isn't like you as a rule but then nobody is perfect!

## 29 SATURDAY          *Moon Age Day 17    Moon Sign Cancer*

The holidays roll on and new input comes from any number of different directions. Listen to what is being said around you because it's quite possible that you can learn something useful.

# 30 SUNDAY

*Moon Age Day 18   Moon Sign Cancer*

You might think that you are in the right about most issues today. That may be true, but there are occasions when it would be sensible to give others the benefit of the doubt.

# 31 MONDAY

*Moon Age Day 19   Moon Sign Leo*

The end of the year brings you to thinking quite deeply about what you have achieved and you will also be carefully planning what comes next. That's fine during the day but by the time the evening arrives you will have other things to do.

# RISING SIGNS FOR TAURUS

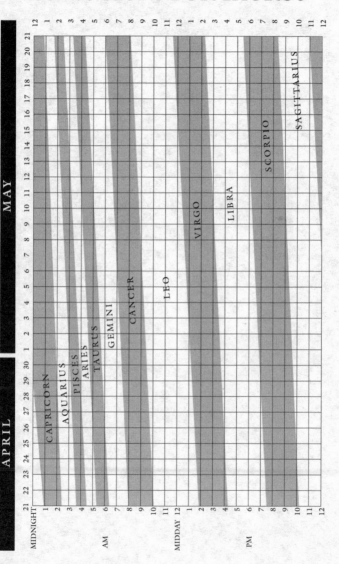

# THE ZODIAC, PLANETS AND CORRESPONDENCES

The Earth revolves around the Sun once every calendar year, so when viewed from Earth the Sun appears in a different part of the sky as the year progresses. In astrology, these parts of the sky are divided into the signs of the zodiac and this means that the signs are organised in a circle. The circle begins with Aries and ends with Pisces.

Taking the zodiac sign as a starting point, astrologers then work with all the positions of planets, stars and many other factors to calculate horoscopes and birth charts and tell us what the stars have in store for us.

The table below shows the planets and Elements for each of the signs of the zodiac. Each sign belongs to one of the four Elements: Fire, Air, Earth or Water. Fire signs are creative and enthusiastic; Air signs are mentally active and thoughtful; Earth signs are constructive and practical; Water signs are emotional and have strong feelings.

It also shows the metals and gemstones associated with, or corresponding with, each sign. The correspondence is made when a metal or stone possesses properties that are held in common with a particular sign of the zodiac.

Finally, the table shows the opposite of each star sign – this is the opposite sign in the astrological circle.

| Placed | Sign | Symbol | Element | Planet | Metal | Stone | Opposite |
|--------|------|--------|---------|--------|-------|-------|----------|
| 1 | Aries | Ram | Fire | Mars | Iron | Bloodstone | Libra |
| 2 | Taurus | Bull | Earth | Venus | Copper | Sapphire | Scorpio |
| 3 | Gemini | Twins | Air | Mercury | Mercury | Tiger's Eye | Sagittarius |
| 4 | Cancer | Crab | Water | Moon | Silver | Pearl | Capricorn |
| 5 | Leo | Lion | Fire | Sun | Gold | Ruby | Aquarius |
| 6 | Virgo | Maiden | Earth | Mercury | Mercury | Sardonyx | Pisces |
| 7 | Libra | Scales | Air | Venus | Copper | Sapphire | Aries |
| 8 | Scorpio | Scorpion | Water | Pluto | Plutonium | Jasper | Taurus |
| 9 | Sagittarius | Archer | Fire | Jupiter | Tin | Topaz | Gemini |
| 10 | Capricorn | Goat | Earth | Saturn | Lead | Black Onyx | Cancer |
| 11 | Aquarius | Waterbearer | Air | Uranus | Uranium | Amethyst | Leo |
| 12 | Pisces | Fishes | Water | Neptune | Tin | Moonstone | Virgo |